A Manual of Monsters & Mythos from Around the World

Rachel Quinney

Andrews McMeel
PUBLISHING®

CRYPTIDS, CREATURES & CRITTERS:
A Manual of Monsters & Mythos from Around the World

Andrews McMeel Publishing
a division of Andrews McMeel Universal
1130 Walnut Street, Kansas City, Missouri 64106

www.andrewsmcmeel.com

24 25 26 27 28 TEN 10 9 8 7 6 5 4 3 2 1

ISBN: 978-1-5248-8983-8

Library of Congress Control Number: 2023949762

Featuring: Bavarii, Caiti Gray, Cory McGowan, Fungii Draws, Giulialibard,
hallalaween, Hari Conner, JuniJwi, Lyndsey Green, Morrighan Corbel,
Rachel Cush, and Tengurine

Editor: Katie Gould
Art Director: Holly Swayne
Production Editor: Elizabeth A. Garcia
Production Manager: Tamara Haus

Attention: Schools and Businesses
Andrews McMeel books are available at quantity discounts with
bulk purchase for educational, business, or sales promotional use.
For information, please e-mail the Andrews McMeel
Publishing Special Sales Department: sales@amuniversal.com.

Kickstarter Edition: In memory of Dillon, the best cat
and cryptid I could ever ask for. A special thanks to all
347 Kickstarter backers who helped bring this project to life
and allowed me to self-publish.

Andrews McMeel Publishing edition: In memory of Ollie,
a gentle and sweet young cat.

CONTENTS

FOLKLORE

MYTHOLOGY

APPENDIXES

INTRODUCTION

It is important to acknowledge that there are clear divisions among cryptids, creatures from folklore, mythological creatures, and creatures within existing religions and cultures.

CRYPTID

The term "cryptid" became popular in the 1990s and is defined as a "creature whose existence or survival is disputed or unsubstantiated."[1] Cryptids are similar to urban legends, stories passed along by word of mouth based on unsubstantiated rumor without religious or mythological origins, stemming from folklore and oral myths.

Cryptids *do not* include creatures such as wendigos or skinwalkers, as they derive from Native American beliefs and have been absorbed into the cryptid community due to a lack of education or willing acceptance to misrepresent their origins. Similarly, some cryptids that have not been lifted from Indigenous beliefs have absorbed racist sentiments into their narrative or physical features due to the fetishization of non-white cultures. One example of this is Mothman, as some sources claim that the area where he was sighted had been "cursed by a Native American chief."[2] There has been a deliberate effort in this book to dismiss or call out stories that echo imperialist narratives or deliberately cherry-pick ideas from Indigenous cultures to make them seem more "mysterious."

FOLKLORE

Folklore and mythology share many similarities. Both are narratives traditionally passed down orally. Folklore tends to be more localized and often focuses on normal individuals overcoming supernatural and otherworldly elements or issuing a warning, moral, or cautionary tale that reflects the culture around them. Folklore rarely deals with the affairs of gods, grand concepts, or issues such as life or death and does not address or present a complex belief system. Creatures of folklore are frequently assumed to be creatures of fantasy and fable and seldom fall under the scrutiny of the scientific community (for example, the repeated investigations into whether the Loch Ness Monster truly exists).

MYTHOLOGY

Mythology and its creatures come from ancient civilizations and have cultural and at times religious significance, usually reflecting conditions or narratives of the era. Mythology deals with similar concepts as folklore but also engages with grander themes, such as creation of mankind, gods, the rules of nature, life, death, and what lies beyond.

Stories within mythology have been changed and corrupted by colonialism. There are multiple monsters whose role has changed to be seen as demonic or evil due to Christian influence, and this book will highlight when external sources have influenced the creature's narrative.

That said, mythology is not solely concerned with the crumbling pantheons of ancient Greece or rotting Viking boats. Some sociologists consider the construction of mythology to be a live and ongoing process, as the stories that we tell each other are used to make sense of the world. For example, the gashadokuro emerged in the 1950s, yet they are considered to be part of Japanese mythology and an urban legend. Perhaps in a century, the Loch Ness Monster will be reassigned from cryptozoology to mythology.

Initially, I wanted to embark on this text through the perspective of an adventurer or scholar who documented the discoveries of these creatures while crossing the globe. The idea swiftly died; the echoes of colonization and imperialism left a sour taste. Instead, this book is more of a series of snapshots, a diving board, a collection of articulate notes for you to pick up the essentials of the creatures while leaving space for you to begin your own research. Ultimately, this book will never rival the narratives told by the people whose cultures originated these tales. As a white woman, it is not my role or right to tell people who live closer to these stories that my word is the truth. In fact, I encourage you to take my writings with a grain of salt. I have done all I can to be as accurate and true to the sources as possible, but no matter how much I research, I will always have more to learn.

HOW TO READ

The book is divided into three sections: "Cryptids," "Folklore," and "Mythology." Within each section, the creatures are labeled alphabetically, allowing you to flip through this book in any order. Many creatures who are arguably very similar or fall under a single category, such as the wolpertinger and the jackalope, are separated. The only exceptions to this are mermaids and plants within folklore. Mermaids have been collected together due to the similarities across narratives, and the plants from folklore due to the limited information available.

Before each description, a creature's region of origin is stated, followed by a classification and content warning.

Classification describes the physical form of the creature.

- A **monster** is anything considered non-humanoid, with more animal or bestial features than humanoid.
- A **spirit** applies to creatures who may have ethereal or ghostly qualities. Spirits include creatures such as ghouls, nymphs, and yokai from Japanese folklore.
- **Humanoids** are beings who are more humanoid than bestial. This includes mermaids, as it is the human qualities that differentiate them from aquatic beasts.
- **Shapeshifters** are creatures who primarily shift between multiple forms. Some creatures will be both humanoid and shapeshifters or both spirits and shapeshifters. They are rarely a singular category.
- Finally, **aliens** are beings believed to come from beyond the stars and who do not have origins here on Earth.

Sometimes these are further broken down into yokai or fae. "Yokai" is a collective term for spirits, specters, demons, and monsters from Japanese folklore. "Fae" describes creatures from the fairy (or "faerie") realm in European folklore.

Some creatures have narratives that involve topics that may be distressing for some readers and, as such, will have content warnings before their descriptions.

A ⭐ by a creature's name signifies that the creature is a singular entity, rather than a species.

Some creatures share interesting overlaps with other monsters or beings that are not in this book. In some descriptions, you will see a note number next to a name. For example:

Interestingly, during the 1800s, mythologists believed Busch-großmutter to be a goddess, rivaling the power and abilities of Frau Holle[5] and Perchta[6].

You can then find a further explanation into these two characters in the Notes section in the back of the book.

While most of the artwork for this book has been drawn by the author, several guest artists have contributed to add a variety of styles and different interpretations of the creatures. On occasion, these guest artists have added their own thoughts and opinions on the creatures that they have drawn, and these appear at the end of the description of the creature. For example:

La says: *Cat sídhe is a creature that in many ways sums up cats exactly . . .*

All the guest artists have been credited at the back of the book (see page 176), where you can find links to their online platforms and enjoy more of their artwork.

CRYPTIDS

BIGFOOT

LOCATION: United States and Canada
CATEGORY: Humanoid

Named in 1958 after his large feet, said to be 16 inches (41 centimeters) long, Bigfoot is one of the most popular and well-known cryptids across the globe and is described as an ape man between 7 and 10 feet (2 and 3 meters) tall with long, powerful arms, covered from head to toe in thick hair.

Sightings of Bigfoot predate the 1840s, with several Indigenous tribes having their own stories and names for the creature. Across the different regions and tribes, his behavior and diet differs, as well as the idea of him being a singular creature or a species.

The Salish people of the First Nations named him (singular) "Sásq'ets," which was anglicized to "Sasquatch" and is now widely considered as an alternative name for Bigfoot (unfortunately, this leads people to ignore the Indigenous history and lore). Depending on the tribe, this giant humanoid has been depicted as a mere gentle creature who coexists with humanity, spiritual guide and teacher, messenger between humanity and animals, or connection to the spiritual world.

In the 1970s, the FBI studied a supposed sample of Bigfoot hair and reported that it belonged to the deer family—however, there are stories out there claiming that the tests came back inconclusive as it took over forty years for the files to be declassified.

Along with Bigfoot, there are a multitude of other hairy humanoid creatures that have appeared across North America in cryptozoology. The Skunk Ape, reported to have a foul fragrance, appeared in the '60s in Florida (I personally like the name "Swamp Cabbage Man" that was given to him). There is the Dewey Lake Monster in Michigan, the Honey Island Swamp Monster in Louisiana, the Mogollon Monster in Arizona, the Fouke Monster in Arkansas, Momo the Monster in Missouri, and Old Yellow Top in Ontario (Canada).

The Bigfoot monster is spread across the globe: Yowie in Australia, Almas in Mongolia, Barmanu in Afghanistan, Yeren in China, Mono Grande in Brazil, and Mande Barung in India. Around the Himalayas, "Bigfoot" has been used interchangeably with "yeti" by Westerners. Stories of yetis can be traced back to the sixth century. The yeti was named the Abominable Snowman in the 1920s by Henry Newman, an English journalist who attempted to translate the native name. He mistranslated "the bearlike snowman" or "the man-bear snowman" as "the filthy snowman." Unimpressed by "the filthy snowman," he took artistic license and referred to the creature as "the abominable snowman."

Bigfoot's narrative has also inspired stories of creatures such as Goatmen (see page 25), Batsquatch, Sheepsquatch, Octosquatch, and many others. The Batsquatch has only been seen once in the 1940s in Washington State. The Sheepsquatch was sighted several times during the 1990s in the state of West Virginia. The Sheepsquatch is the size of a large bear; it's covered in white fur and has two large ram horns on its head. Unlike many of the creatures under the Bigfoot umbrella, the Sheepsquatch has a long, skin-colored tail like a possum and omits a sulfurous odor. The Octosquatch was sighted in 1961 in northern Spain and stands at approximately 4 to 5 feet (about 1.3 meters) tall. Described as a humanoid octopus covered in hair, one can only imagine the smell that this cryptid must emit!

CACTUS CAT

LOCATION: Southwestern United States
CATEGORY: Plant monster
CONTENT WARNING: Alcohol

Sightings of cactus cats were first reported in the American Southwest as pioneers spread across the land. A cactus cat is noticeably different from a jaguar or bobcat due to the large spines protruding from its body. Cactus cats have multiple subspecies and mimic different species of cacti; some are said to have floral growths. One interpretation of the cactus cat imagines its tail to be shaped like a ball and chain.

The cactus cat is said to walk long distances, cutting open cacti with its knifelike claws as it travels. It resists the cactus juice but returns days later to the opened cacti, whose sap has now fermented, and feasts on the intoxicating juice. The cactus cat will drink until it is full and inebriated before staggering out into the desert, announcing its presence to the world with loud shrieks.

The cactus cat sleeps during the day to avoid the desert heat inside the husk of a carved-out cacti. Male cactus cats attract a mate by cutting open a saguaro cactus and, tempted by the scent of the cactus juice, a female will often fight other females to the death before getting drunk with the male cat. Within weeks, a litter of cactus kittens will be born.

Fun fact: It is generally accepted that they are immune to scorpion venom.

CANVEY ISLAND MONSTER

LOCATION: Canvey Island, England, United Kingdom
CATEGORY: Monster

A mysterious carcass washed up on the shore of Canvey Island in November 1953. It was just over 30 inches (76 centimeters) long with a body that resembled a fish and had thick, red skin and bulbous eyes, but the most unusual thing about this aquatic creature was that it appeared to have hind legs and feet. Zoologists sent to investigate this creature did not reach a conclusion as to the creature's identity and subsequently cremated the remains.

Less than a year later, in August 1954, a larger specimen washed up in much better condition than the first. The second carcass measured 47 inches (120 centimeters) long and had a large, gaping maw filled with needlelike teeth. There were distinct nostrils and gills on the second corpse, and the skin was tough and thick. The feet were in better condition, allowing scientists to note that it had five toes on each foot. Both carcasses are considered types of globsters (see page 23).

Zoologists theorize that the Canvey Island Monsters may be washed up anglerfish, and the distinct toes of the monster may be frayed fins. Others say it is a monkfish, while some argue it may be a frogfish, a species that walks on its hind fins. During the 1950s, there was speculation that it may be a prehistoric monster, as the rediscovery of the coelacanth, once thought extinct, had happened less than twenty years earlier.

CHUPACABRA

LOCATION: Puerto Rico
CATEGORY: Monster
CONTENT WARNING: Animal death

Stories of the Chupacabra originated in the 1990s from Puerto Rico when the bodies of eight sheep were discovered drained of blood, each bearing three puncture wounds in their chest. In the following months, over 150 farm animals and pets were found in similar conditions. Once the narrative of the Chupacabra began, similar styles of killings that had happened fifteen years prior in 1975, previously thought to be by El Vampiro de Moca ("The Vampire of Moca"), were attributed to the Chupacabra.

The tales of "El Chupacabra," a bipedal reptilian creature that jumped like a kangaroo, began to spread, along with reports of sightings throughout 1995. It is reported to be about the size of a bear with large spines stretching from the base of the neck to the tail—this is the Puerto Rican Chupacabra. During the 2000s, sightings of the Chupacabra were reported in Texas, but the description changed to a strange hairless dog with a pronounced ridged spine, exaggerated eye sockets, large claws, and three triangular-shaped fangs used to drain blood. It is believed that the hound-like sightings of Chupacabras are coyotes and dogs suffering from mange. Thus, there are two types of Chupacabra: the Puerto Rican reptilian Chupacabra and the Texan dog Chupacabra. The rise of Texan Chupacabra sightings and the number of mistakenly identified dead dogs and coyotes transformed the cultural beliefs of Texans (and, later, the world) that the Chupacabra was a species rather than a singular creature like the Puerto Rican Chupacabra.

Chupacabra translates from Spanish as "to suck" (*chupar*) and "goat" (*cabra*). Science has found little evidence to prove the existence of the cryptid. Dogs with mange grow thin and weak and begin to lose fur; they become desperate for food and may attack livestock. The startled bitten goat dashes for its life, only to die later of internal hemorrhaging. When the body is later examined, it does not "spurt blood," as blood thickens and coagulates after death, giving the illusion of being drained of blood. The appearance of the Chupacabra began to be linked with the now-extinct thylacine, or Tasmanian tiger—perhaps out of hope that the creature had not gone extinct.

CRAWFORDSVILLE MONSTER ⭐

LOCATION: Crawfordsville, Indiana, United States
CATEGORY: Alien

On September 5, 1891, two delivery men reported witnessing an extraterrestrial phenomenon in the sky. A long specter about 16 feet (5 meters) long and 6.5 feet (2 meters) wide writhed above them like a large, white shroud. They described seeing fins that propelled the creature; there was no visible head, tail, or mouth, but they did see a single large, flaming red eye. It twisted in the sky as if in agony, releasing a low, wheezing wail, and emitted "hot breath" over those who stood beneath it.

At the time, people wondered whether it was a monster, an alien, or a ghost, but three days later, the monster appeared again. Two different witnesses followed the wraith across town and discovered that the creature was really a flock of killdeer, small birds with white on their bellies and wings. The birds were distressed and disoriented after the installation of electric lights. The Crawfordsville Monster inspired the school of thought that aliens may be microscopic or gaseous creatures.

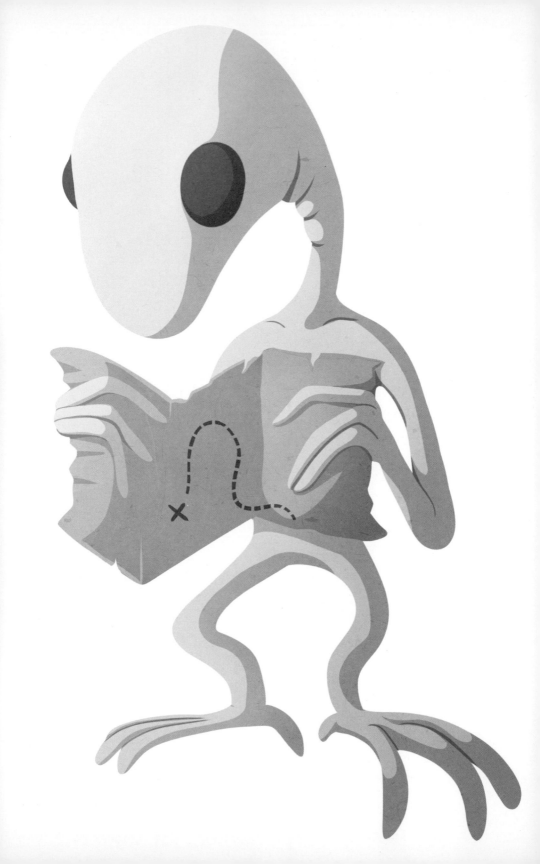

DOVER DEMON ⊛

LOCATION: Dover, Massachusetts, United States
CATEGORY: Alien

Spotted in Dover, Massachusetts, on April 21 and 22, 1977, the Dover Demon had a large, melon-shaped head, an emaciated, scrawny body, and long, tendril-like fingers. It stood at just over 4 feet (1.2 meters) tall and had large, glowing orange eyes (one witness claimed they were green) and did not have a mouth or nose.

The Dover Demon was witnessed three times by four different individuals over the two nights. All sightings took place near water less than two miles apart; strangely, when plotted on a map, they appeared in a straight line. Critics are dubious about the Dover Demon's existence as the witnesses were teenagers, but to this day, the main witness, William Bartlett, still insists that the sighting was genuine. Some critics suggest that the Dover Demon may have been a misidentified baby moose; however, moose are unlikely to walk on their hind legs or sit on a wall, as witnesses of the Dover Demon reported.

ENFIELD HORROR ⭐

LOCATION: Enfield, Illinois, United States
CATEGORY: Monster

Not to be confused with the Enfield Poltergeist (London, United Kingdom), the Enfield Horror struck in 1973 in Enfield, Illinois. A scratching sound drew Henry McDaniel outside his house, where he shot at a creature that he initially believed to be a bear until he pulled a flashlight out. The Enfield Horror is covered in gray fur and has a short thick body, three legs (each foot with six toes), two short arms ending in claws, and two giant pink eyes. It stands just over 4 feet (1.2 meters) tall and shrieks like a wildcat. Despite its cumbersome appearance, it moves very quickly.

The Enfield Horror leaves behind footprints, with two prints side by side and the third foot marginally in front and slightly smaller. The Enfield Horror has been compared to the Mount Vernon Monster (witnessed in 1942) as they both produce loud shrieking noises and hop or jump like a kangaroo to travel. The creature has not been seen since the series of sightings in 1973, but many believe that the Horror is still out there.

FLATHEAD LAKE MONSTER ⭐

LOCATION: Flathead Lake, Montana, United States
CATEGORY: Monster

The Flathead Lake Monster is an elusive aquatic cryptid found in Flathead Lake in Montana. Nicknamed "Montana Nessie" or "Flossie," the Flathead Lake Monster is one of many water-based cryptids that share similarities with the Loch Ness Monster (see page 37).

The Flathead Lake Monster has two physical descriptions, which suggests that there may be more than one type of creature in the deep lake. One has the head of a snake and an eellike body that could be as long as 40 feet (12 meters). The second variant is often much smaller at about 10 feet (3 meters) and frequently matches the description of a large sturgeon, a rather angular looking freshwater fish. This second variant of the Flathead Lake Monster is sometimes described to have a large dorsal fin.

The Flathead Lake Monster was first sighted in 1889 by Captain James C. Kerr. While he was sailing his passenger boat, he spotted a 20-foot (6-meter) shadow moving under the water. One of the passengers fired a rifle at the creature, but his shot missed, and the creature disappeared down into the depths. Another strange creature described as a giant dog was spotted in the lake in 1937. In 1949, a family spotted a giant creature rising to the surface and descending again, but the father of the family suspected it to be a 12-foot (3.7-meter) sturgeon. In 1955, the Gilbert family spotted two large creatures playing in the water. A decade later, in 1965, the Funke family spotted a large black dorsal fin approaching their boat—after passing, it created a significant wake. In 1985, an army major and his son witnessed a long eellike creature and saw it again two years later. The Flathead Lake Monster was also seen in 1993 by the Gaffney family, who described it as "Nessie-like," approximately 20 feet (6 meters) long with large humps. Other hump-based sightings were recorded in 1998 and 2005; the latter sighting reported to see six of them swimming together.

FLATWOODS MONSTER ★

LOCATION: Flatwoods, West Virginia, United States
CATEGORY: Alien

The Flatwoods Monster has many names: the Braxton County Monster, the Green Monster, the Phantom of Flatwoods, or Braxy. On September 12, 1952, multiple people witnessed an oval-shaped ball of fire shoot across the sky over Flatwoods and descend toward a nearby farm. Five witnesses headed toward Fisher Farm to investigate further. They climbed to the top of a hill, where they were greeted by a red, pulsating light, the overpowering stench of sulfur, a strange mist, a shrill, metallic whining sound, and a 10-foot- (3-meter-) tall alien.

The head was shaped like the ace of spades, with a bloodred face and large yellow eyes. It had clawed hands and a greenish or dark body, which gave off a faint glow. Mrs. May, one of the initial witnesses, described the creature to have "drape-like folds." The eyes cast beams of light where they looked. Upon seeing the group, the monster hissed and began to float toward them, causing them to flee. When police explored the landing site later on, they found unusual skid marks and an "odd, gummy deposit."

Many of the people who witnessed the monster or entered the location shortly after its arrival fell sick with symptoms of mustard gas poisoning, and it is believed it may have been caused by inhaling the bizarre mist. Many believe the alien craft to have simply been a meteor. Other skeptics believe the Flatwoods Monster to be nothing more than a panicked barn owl seen in poor lighting by hysterical individuals, as the monster's hood mirrors the shape of a barn owl face, talons could have been mistaken for claws, and the movements of a startled barn owl are strange to people who are unfamiliar with barn owl behavior. Despite the skeptics, there is a yearly festival held in Flatwoods to celebrate the Flatwoods Monster's visit.

FRESNO NIGHTCRAWLERS

LOCATION: Fresno, California, United States
CATEGORY: Alien

The Fresno Nightcrawlers or Fresno Nightwalkers are comically referred to as "walking trousers" or "walking teeth" (the latter is far more upsetting as a concept). Fresno Nightcrawlers are predominantly legs with no arms or body and, despite their name, do not crawl. Witnesses vary on how tall the aliens are, with some reports stating that they are over 7 feet (2 meters) tall, some at 3 feet (1 meter), and some at 1.5 feet (46 centimeters) tall; however, all confirm the creatures are either white or pale gray.

Fresno Nightcrawlers have always appeared in pairs and have been caught on CCTV and by a handheld camera. They appear to be benevolent, causing no harm to the viewer. There have been multiple attempts to mimic the walking pattern of these creatures, from puppetry to costuming. Some attempts have proven that certain evidence are hoaxes, whereas others have failed to mimic the bizarre walk.

Many theorize that Fresno Nightcrawlers and the Carmel Area Creature in Ohio are the same species.

GEROTA ⭐

LOCATION: The Catlins, New Zealand
CATEGORY: Monster

Supposedly found in caves in the Catlins, a gerota is a hybrid of a bat and a possum. The cryptid was discovered by Lester Rowntree, who displayed a taxidermied gerota in 2011 to entice locals to visit his heritage farm show. The gerota on display is widely believed to be a chimera of different animal body parts sewn together, leaving many in the cryptozoology community to believe it is a hoax.

A gerota is described to have the body of a possum with a long, dark, and fluffy tail. It has a pair of large bat-like wings, two horns on its head, and noticeable fangs protruding from its mouth. One could argue that the gerota is a type of wolpertinger (see page 57).

GLOBSTER

LOCATION: Worldwide
CATEGORY: Monster
CONTENT WARNING: Animal death

A globster is an unidentified rotting carcass that has washed ashore. Although the term was coined in 1962 by Ivan Sanderson, globsters have been reported as far back as 1648. Due to decomposition in the ocean as well as the corpse being a source of food for marine life, many washed-up bodies of marine animals are no longer recognizable by the time they reach the beach. Before DNA testing, globsters were a source of great speculation, with people believing them to be an entirely new species and some cultures associating the appearance of a globster with an omen of bad fortune.

Globsters have been described as white and often covered with fibers. They have no discernable eyes, no bone structure, and have a rubbery or stringy texture. Modern globsters have been identified as the remains of large aquatic life, such as whales, basking sharks, oarfish, and squids; however, historical cases of globsters are yet to be solved.[3]

GOATMAN

LOCATION: Maryland, Texas, Kentucky, and Pennsylvania, United
States
CATEGORY: Humanoid
CONTENT WARNING: Animal death, historic racism and lynching,
bestiality

Considered more of an urban legend than a cryptid, the Goatman has
different narratives among the four states he is supposed to reside in.
Cryptozoologists debate whether there is a singular Goatman who has
traveled among the four states or whether the Goatman is part of a
species (Goatmen). Descriptions of the Goatman's appearance are the
same across the states: He has the head of a goat, the torso of a human,
the lower body of a goat, is covered in fur, and has great red eyes.
There are similarities between the physical features of the Goatman
and the Sheepsquatch (see page 4). The Goatman's appearance parallels that of the ancient Greek satyrs.

Maryland: The Maryland Goatman is said to be the result of
a scientific experiment gone wrong at the Beltsville Agricultural
Research Center. Stories tell of a scientist who was transformed into
a savage Goatman with an insatiable craving for blood. With an axe in
hand, he stalks the roads of Beltsville. His only known victim is a puppy
named Ginger, whose decapitated head was found near Fletchertown
Road in 1971. The Goatman is believed to lurk near lovers' lane in search
of victims and has supposedly mauled several cars.

Texas: Unlike the other Goatman stories, the Texas Goatman is
described to have scales as well as fur. He was sighted in 1969 near
Lake Worth, giving it the name "Lake Worth Monster." According to
contemporary newspapers, he pounced on a parked car, attempting
to grab the woman inside. The car sped away, but not before receiving
an 18-inch (46-centimeter) slash across its bodywork. He appeared on a
cliffside the following day while people were dumping rubbish into the
lake and threw a tire a distance of five hundred feet toward the crowd.

Another version of the Goatman from Texas revolves around
"Goatman's Bridge," or Old Alton Bridge, as it is officially named. First

sightings date back to 1938. The Goatman is believed to appear if you cross the bridge alone at night on foot or if you drive across without headlights on. Supposedly, if you honk your horn twice at midnight, only his eyes appear, watching you from the darkness. People have reported hearing voices and hooves on the bridge at night. There are countless tales of the bridge, including rumors of supposedly abandoned cars with owners who have mysteriously disappeared, and in another story, witnesses stated that they had seen the ghost of a shepherd guiding his goats over the bridge. The surrounding woods also host a collection of spooky and dangerous tales.

There are two well-known origin stories for this Goatman. One is that Satanists performed a ritual that summoned the beast from another realm (bridges are often considered gateways to other realms). The more famous version states that the bridge was used by the Ku Klux Klan to lynch a successful Black businessman named Oscar Washburn, who traded goats and referred to himself as "the Goatman" on a business sign. It is believed that his spirit haunts the bridge; however, there are no documents proving Oscar's existence.

Kentucky: Named the "Pope Lick Monster" after Pope Lick Creek, this Goatman has never been actually sighted. The Pope Lick Monster is said to use hypnosis or vocal mimicry to lure victims onto the bridge and into the path of oncoming trains. Other stories state that he wields a bloody axe or that his very presence drives those who see him to leap over the edge of the bridge to their deaths. The Pope Lick Monster has tasteless origin stories, some stating that he is a "circus freak," the offspring of a farmer and his goat, or that he is the reincarnation of a farmer who sacrificed his goats for power.

Pennsylvania: Originally called the Waterford Sheepman, this Goatman appeared in the 1970s near a bridge. He was seen darting from the road into the brush on multiple occasions. One local stated that the Waterford Sheepman would hide in the rafters of the bridge, waiting for lovers to pull up in their car, before jumping down to scare them away.

HODAG ⭐

LOCATION: Rhinelander, Wisconsin, United States
CATEGORY: Monster

The first sighting was in 1893 in Rhinelander, Wisconsin, by a well-known local prankster, Eugene Shepard, who circulated photographic evidence to rally a hunting party. According to the story, the Hodag failed to be harmed by weapons but was bested by dynamite. Three years later, Shepard claimed to have caught a live Hodag and displayed the creature in a darkened tent; however, he later admitted that it was made of wood and leather and that he made it move by using wires.

The original Hodag was described to be 7 feet (2 meters) long and 2.5 feet (70 centimeters) tall, weighing around 200 pounds (91 kilograms). Shepard said it was covered in fur and had the large face of a grinning, fanged frog, thick legs with long claws, and spikes all along its back and tail.

While the Hodag is considered to be a hoax by most, it has been adopted locally as a mascot for sports teams and is a town icon in Rhinelander. Rhinelander officials state that the Hodag has delicious lemonade tears (but never cries), uses its tail to roast marshmallows, and can listen to the local radio using its large horns as antennas. The Hodag apparently smells like fresh pine and once did a cannon-ball jump into a puddle, forming Boom Lake. The Hodag is blamed for stolen golf balls, missing keys, and mislaid glasses and is accused of swiping food and stealing "the big one" from local fishers. It's all tongue in cheek, but the Hodag is quite an amusing little fellow and is a source of tourism income to the local community.

HOOP SNAKE

LOCATION: United States and Canada
CATEGORY: Monster

The hoop snake is a cryptid that has been seen across the United States, from Texas to Minnesota, and up into Canada. The bright and colorful hoop snake bites its own tail, turning it into a hoop or wheel, and then rolls toward its victims, reaching speeds of up to 60 mph (97 kmph). Hoop snakes are incredibly venomous and have sharp prongs on the end of their tail that they use to stab their victims. It is believed the venom from a hoop snake can cause a mature tree to wither, blacken, and die within twenty-four hours.

The hoop snake is physically similar to Ouroboros, the image of a snake devouring its own tail that symbolizes the cycle of life and death, dating back to 1400 BCE. Another creature that could have inspired the hoop snake is the Tsuchinoko, a snake from Japanese folklore that can also bite its own tail and move by rolling. However, it is more likely that the hoop snake was inspired by mud snakes, which form hoops with their bodies and use their tails to prod prey.

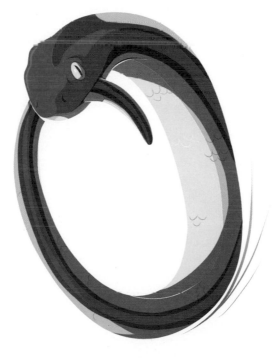

HOPKINSVILLE GOBLINS

LOCATION: Near Kelly and Hopkinsville, Kentucky, United States
CATEGORY: Alien

On August 21, 1955, at around 7 PM, a light soared over the Sutton farmhouse (seven miles north of Hopkinsville) and descended into a nearby gully with a sharp hissing noise, a thin stream of prismatic smoke pouring from the exhaust of their spaceship. The witness reported the sight to his family, who dismissed him, saying it was a shooting star. When the dog started barking an hour later, the family looked outside to see (as was later named) the Hopkinsville goblins approaching the house with raised claws.

The goblins were 3 feet (1 meter) tall, each with a large head and yellow glowing eyes that were set far apart. Their big ears were floppy, like leather. They had short bodies, long arms, and at the end of each hand, several talons. They were a luminescent silver or metal-clad and floated as they approached the farmhouse.

The family fired at the goblins with rifles and shotguns, but the bullets did no damage and bounced off. The impact caused the goblins to fall backward in the air, flip back up, and resume floating toward the family. The family fled from the farmhouse to Hopkinsville, reporting the incident to local police, who investigated the scene for over five hours but saw no evidence to prove or disprove the goblins' presence. Half an hour after the officials left, the goblins returned, tormenting the family until sunrise before departing. It is believed that they have an aversion to light.

The story of the Hopkinsville goblins is often considered not credible, as the witnesses were rural farmers and carnival workers and deemed unreliable due to prejudices and stereotypes about their employment and lifestyles. In addition, the media were not concerned with accurately reporting the story. As a result, the goblins are thought of as little green men even though the goblins were silver. Later descriptions by the media added scales and feathers to the goblins. Despite the sighting being considered fake, Hopkinsville celebrates the aliens with the neighboring community, Kelly, with the Kelly Little Green Men Days Festival every August.

Fun fact: The Pokémon Sableye was inspired by the Hopkinsville goblins.

JACKALOPE

LOCATION: Southwestern United States
CATEGORY: Monster

The word "jackalope" derives from "jackrabbit" and "antelope"; however, jackalopes are a hybrid of various species of hares, with the horns of a deer or pronghorn (pronghorns are colloquially referred to as "antelopes"). Jackalopes can grow to 4 feet (1.2 meters) in height and reach speeds of 60 to 90 mph (97 to 145 kmph) while running.

Jackalopes are extremely territorial and aggressive, using their horns to gore anyone who enters their territory. Despite this, they are widely hunted for their milk, which has aphrodisiac qualities or medicinal powers, depending on the source. According to folklore, the most effective way to milk a jackalope is to give it whiskey, as all jackalopes adore the taste and it will quickly become intoxicated. After that, they are much slower and easier to milk.

Not only are they lightning fast, carriers of magical milk, and whisky connoisseurs but jackalopes are also able to mimic the sounds of humans and echo their singing around a campfire at night. Some tales recount how a jackalope can throw its voice, making it harder to track and catch by throwing hunters off its trail. Jackalopes become more verbally active before a thunderstorm and will only mate during flashes of lightning.

There are several creatures within folklore that share a similar appearance to the jackalope. The raurakl can be found in Austria (though there is very little information about the raurakl). In addition, you can find hares with the antlers of a roe deer and sharp canine-like teeth in south Germany named the rasselbock. Jackalopes are also compared to the Hessian dilldapp, which is a hamster with antlers and sometimes wings—linking it to the wolpertinger (see page 57).

JERSEY DEVIL ⭐

LOCATION: New Jersey, United States
CATEGORY: Monster

In 1735, Deborah Leeds discovered she was pregnant with her thirteenth child and, in her frustration and distress, cursed the unborn child to be a devil. When the thirteenth child was born, it was born with horns, bat wings, and a devil's tail. Startled by the cramped conditions it was born into, it began to snarl and shriek before flying up the chimney and fleeing into the Pine Barrens. One variation on the story states that Leeds was actually a witch, and the father of the child was the Devil; however, there is evidence of a Leeds family in 1735 with twelve children.

In the 1840s, the Jersey Devil was blamed for numerous sheep killings. In 1909, the Jersey Devil was frequently sighted across the state. Sightings included seeing the beast attack a trolley bus, hunters spotting the beast while on patrol, and locals discovering unidentified footprints in the snow. In 1925, a farmer claimed to have shot the Jersey Devil, and in 1937, 1951, and 1957, the Jersey Devil was spotted again by multiple witnesses. In 1960, more unidentified tracks were linked to the Jersey Devil. The local zoo offered a reward for anyone who could capture the beast; however, all they received were numerous hoaxes, including a kangaroo with fake claws and bat wings. In 1961, a car was attacked by a screeching, winged beast in the Pine Barrens. Sightings dramatically increased from 1960 to 1980, along with a rise in animal mutilations.

The Jersey Devil's description, based on the 1909 sightings, is 8.5 feet (2.6 meters) tall with a long neck, a horse's face, and two horns. It has a pair of large bat wings, two short front legs with paws on the end, two long hind legs (like a crane) with hooves, and a forked tail. A less popular description states that it has long black hair, monkey hands, a doglike face, split hooves, and a tail. Some theorize that the Jersey Devil may actually be a sandhill crane, which has a wingspan of 7 feet (2 meters).

LOCH NESS MONSTER ⭐

LOCATION: Scotland, United Kingdom
CATEGORY: Monster

The Loch Ness Monster, sometimes lovingly referred to as "Nessie," lives in Loch Ness in Scotland. After the first sighting in 1933, thousands have flocked to Scotland in hopes of catching a glimpse of the elusive beast. Nessie is described to be between 10 feet and 45 feet long (3 meters and 14 meters) with dark-brown or black skin. There are two popular versions of Nessie's appearance. One resembles a plesiosaur and has an orb-like body, four long fins to propel herself through the water (or waddle on land like a seal), and a long neck like a submarine periscope. An alternative compares her to an eel with fins, allowing her to create the famous "hump" imagery associated with her.

Several photos of Nessie have been revealed as hoaxes, but that has not stopped the world from theorizing on what she could be. Theories have included a line of swimming elephants, a plump of seals, a group of swimming deer, a flock of birds, a school of catfish, a shiver of Greenland sharks, a plesiosaur or a similar prehistoric creature, a giant eel, a long-necked newt, wakes caused by boats, optical illusions, fallen trees, or seismic gas.

Similar to Bigfoot, stories of lake monsters like Nessie have appeared all over the world.[4]

LUSCA

LOCATION: Bahamas
CATEGORY: Monster
CONTENT WARNING: Death

The Lusca lives in blue holes in the ocean around the Bahamas. Blue holes are sinkholes that have formed beneath the ocean and create a vast network of caves and tunnels that are mostly unexplored. The Lusca is a large, oceanic beast that varies in size from 72 to 197 feet (22 to 60 meters) long. It has been described as a giant octopus, half shark and half eel, half shark and half octopus, or as an enormous eel. It has giant phosphorescent eyes.

The Lusca surfaces on full moons and has been blamed for numerous diving deaths in the blue holes, disappearing fishing boats, and incidents of individuals vanishing near the shore line. Divers have reported seeing sharks snatched into the depths by large tentacles. One sailing crew reported buoys being dragged underwater and a large triangular shape appearing on sonar. When they finally retrieved the buoys, they had taken significant damage.

One theory explaining this monster says that tidal surges and vortexes may be mistaken for tentacles. Due to the complicated nature of documenting the many tunnels and the sheer depth of blue holes, it invites human imagination to run wild.

MONGOLIAN DEATH WORM

LOCATION: Gobi Desert, Mongolia and China
CATEGORY: Monster

Originally named *olgoi-khorkhoi,* meaning "large intestine worm," the Mongolian Death Worm is a bloodred worm approximately as long as a large intestine, 2 to 7 feet (61 centimeters to 2 meters), with large spikes at each end of its body. The worm has no distinct eyes, and there is no agreement over whether or not it has a mouth. The Mongolian Death Worm travels underground in order to surprise its prey and uses a variety of lethal attacks: It can spray thick, bubbling acidic poison or give off deadly electric shocks; just touching the beast leaves the victim in an incredible amount of pain. Not only does the Mongolian Death Worm prey on humans but it will also lay eggs inside the stomachs of camels. The Mongolian Death Worm hibernates for the majority of the year, only waking between June and July.

The Mongolian Death Worm was unheard of in the Western world until 1926, when Roy Chapman Andrews published *On the Trail of Ancient Man,* which featured a secondhand account of the creature. It can be found in the Gobi Desert near where goyo plants grow. Speculations on the authenticity of the worm vary; some suggest it could be an overgrown earthworm or a large lizard worm—however, those rarely grow over 6 inches (15 centimeters). Another possible theory is that the Mongolian Death Worm is an amalgamation of the electric eel and a spitting cobra, and its story is used to caution individuals about the venomous snakes in the Gobi Desert.

MONTAUK MONSTER ⊛

LOCATION: Montauk, New York, United States
CATEGORY: Monster
CONTENT WARNING: Animal death

The Montauk Monster washed ashore in Montauk, New York, in 2008 and set the internet on fire with speculation. The gray, fleshy creature that resembled a dog with a beak created a multitude of theories as to its origin. Theories included a raccoon, a shell-less sea turtle, a large rodent, or a coyote. However, multiple individuals highlighted the short distance between the corpse and the Plum Island Animal Disease Center, fueling speculation that the creature was an "experiment gone rogue."

While many scientists believe that the Montauk Monster is just a raccoon, the corpse mysteriously vanished within twenty-four hours of discovery and has not been seen since. The Montauk Monster has been categorized as a globster (see page 23), despite doubts that it came from the ocean.

MOTHMAN ⭐

LOCATION: Point Pleasant, West Virginia, United States
CATEGORY: Humanoid
CONTENT WARNING: Death

First sighted in the winter of 1966, Mothman terrorized the town and surrounding areas of Point Pleasant, West Virginia. He was first witnessed by a group of gravediggers as he swooped over the graveyard. Three days later, on November 15, Mothman was seen again by two couples from inside a car as he lurked around an abandoned generator plant. Distressed by the sight, the driver revved the engine and sped off in the car; however, that was when the Mothman took flight and chased the car, keeping up with it as it drove over 70 mph (113 kmph). It was only when the car reached the city limits that Mothman gave up the chase. Mothman was seen in the same spot the following night and then multiple times over the following year, usually in the same area. The lands and forest surrounding the generator plant are colloquially referred to as the "TNT Area," as explosives were manufactured and stored in concrete igloos in the area during World War II. After the war ended, the explosives were no longer required, and the area was abandoned and left for wildlife. Some individuals speculate that Mothman may have been "born" from the waste materials or that he was drawn to the location for its secluded nature and the absence of humans.

On December 15, 1967, Point Pleasant's Silver Bridge collapsed into the river, resulting in forty-six fatalities. Investigators blamed the accident on erosion and fatigue on the bridge's suspension; however, people began to speculate about Mothman's involvement. It is theorized that Mothman may be a harbinger of doom, warning people that a disaster is approaching. After the collapse, people stated that Mothman had been witnessed near Silver Bridge in the days leading up to the collapse; however, this may be an attempt at historical editing. This narrative was popularized through *The Mothman Prophecies,* a book published in 1975 by John Keel and then adapted into a film in 2002.

Mothman stands at 5 to 7 feet (1.5 to 2 meters) tall. He is broader than an average man and has no arms and a 10-foot (3-meter) wingspan. He is black or gray with a pair of glowing red eyes. Despite the name Mothman, he is rarely described to have mothlike wings and is often depicted with feathery or bat wings. According to witnesses, he does not need to flap his wings to take off or fly, and he shuffles or waddles across the ground while walking. He is described as making shrill noises.

Skeptics theorize that Mothman may be a sandhill crane, a turkey vulture, or a large species of owl. Regardless, Point Pleasant has embraced Mothman with a museum and yearly festival to celebrate the beloved cryptid.

NINGEN ⭐

LOCATION: Southern Ocean, around Antarctica
CATEGORY: Humanoid

First sighted by Japanese fishermen in 1990, the Ningen floated alongside their boat, shimmering in the moonlight, before quietly submerging back into the depths. The Ningen was virtually unheard of until 2007, when an internet thread was discovered by a paranormal-focused magazine in Japan. This publication led to the Ningen's rise in popularity in cryptozoology circles.

The Ningen is a large, white humanoid with blubbery skin similar to a whale and long human limbs (some describe the Ningen to have fins attached to its arms). The creature has two large black eyes and a thin, slit-like mouth. The first Ningen sighting described the creature to be 90 feet (27 meters) long; however, sightings since have ranged between 20 feet and 90 feet (6 meters and 27 meters).

Skeptics believe the Ningen to be a block of floating ice or a misidentified albino whale or stingray.

OWLMAN ⭐

LOCATION: Cornwall, England, United Kingdom
CATEGORY: Humanoid

Considered the English equivalent of Mothman, the Owlman first appeared in 1976 hovering above a church tower in the village of Mawnan in south Cornwall. Sightings of the Owlman continued around the church for the following twenty-five years. While the Owlman has mostly been seen flying, one of the most notable sightings reported him walking through the woods near the forest. Upon noticing that the witness had seen him, he hissed and took flight.

The Owlman is between 4 feet and 7 feet (1.2 meters and 2 meters) tall with a wingspan of 10 feet (3 meters). He has large, glowing red eyes, pointed ears, a black beak, clawed wings, black legs with large taloned feet, and is covered in silver and gray feathers.

The paranormal expert who collated and documented sightings of the Owlman has been accused of creating him as a hoax. Others point out that church towers are popular nesting grounds for owls and speculate that the Owlman is just a large, misidentified long-eared owl or Eurasian eagle owl.

ROD

LOCATION: Roswell, New Mexico, United States—now worldwide
CATEGORY: Alien

Rods, also called "air rods" or "sky fish," are unexplained aerial phenomena that cannot be witnessed by the naked eye and can only be viewed by slow-motion camera replay, as they move so quickly. While they were initially seen at Roswell, which is famous for the Roswell grays abduction (see page 49), sightings have become far more commonplace since the 1990s. Rods are typically white lines, like a string or rope, moving in a straight line or in a rapid spiraling motion. Many skeptics speculate that rods are actually lens flares or insects, dust, or clouds that have been distorted due to motion blur.

ROSWELL GRAYS

LOCATION: Roswell, New Mexico, and New Hampshire, United
States
CATEGORY: Alien
CONTENT WARNING: Sexual assault

A flying disc crashed at a ranch in Roswell, New Mexico, in 1947. The military stated that it was a weather balloon; however, in the 1970s, ufologists began to doubt the truth behind the statement.

On July 3, 1947, the flying disc was seen over the Foster ranch before exploding and crashing to the ground. The craft left a 500-foot-(152-meter-) long gouge in the earth, and despite the gouge not being very deep, the heat from the craft collision had turned the sandy ground around it into glass (causing the Roswell Incident to be one of the only alien encounters to leave physical evidence). The explosion showered an area of three-quarters of a mile (1.2 kilometers) in debris and supposedly ejected two bodies from the ship as it hurtled toward the earth. These two bodies were supposedly of gray aliens.

On the evening of September 19, 1961, Betty and Barney Hill were abducted from their car as they drove through New Hampshire at night. They reported seeing the craft move erratically across the night sky before it began chasing their car. The couple lost consciousness until the next morning, and with no recollection of the events of the night, they returned home. At home, both felt compelled to examine their genitals before taking long showers and falling asleep. Betty noticed that her dress was torn at the hem, lining, and zipper, as well as dusted with a strange pink powder. In addition, the car they had been driving was marked with concentric circles that had their own magnetic field.

For five nights, Betty experienced intense dreams that many believe were memories of the event. She recalled being thoroughly examined and communicating with the aliens. She describes them as being gray-skinned with blueish lips, large black eyes, distinct noses, and having black hair on their heads. They all wore a blue military-style uniform, and were about 5 feet, 4 inches (1.56 meters) tall.

When undergoing hypnotherapy, Betty's accounts were very similar to her dreams though with some variations on her capture and release. Barney's hypnotherapy results were similar though he recalled the aliens using telepathy to communicate with them.

The gray aliens, or "grays," of the Barney and Betty Hill abduction became synonymous with aliens and extraterrestrial life. Ufologists linked the grays with the Roswell incident years later based on testimonial evidence of the bodies thrown from the craft by civilians.

SKVADER

LOCATION: Sweden
CATEGORY: Monster

Considered the Swedish cousin of the jackalope (see page 33) and wolpertinger (see page 57), the skvader is a winged rabbit first discovered in 1874 by a hunter who preserved and stuffed the body (it is still on display today). The skvader is a cross between a hare and a wood grouse, with some versions giving it the tail of a grouse. Scholars frequently cite Pliny the Elder's (23 to 79 CE) description of a creature with a bird's body and rabbit's head to support the skvader and its potential existence.

SNALLYGASTER ⭐

LOCATION: Maryland, United States
CATEGORY: Monster
CONTENT WARNING: Historical racism and discussion of slavery

The Snallygaster began to torment a settlement of German immigrants during the 1730s by silently swooping down and carrying children and livestock off into the night. The Snallygaster has vampiric qualities and drains its victims of blood. Its shriek sounds like the whistle of a locomotive (however, the shrieking noise could have been local moonshiners trying to prevent people from getting too close to their noisy stills). In 1909, Snallygaster fever struck Maryland when the local paper reported a string of sightings and offered a significant reward for the creature's body, even piquing the interest of President Theodore Roosevelt. However, many noted that these sightings shared similarities with reports of the Jersey Devil (see page 35) that had happened weeks earlier.

Often compared to a dragon, the Snallygaster is a large winged monster with a metal beak, feathered wings, a reptilian body, and sharp, hooklike silver claws. Later reports added that the beast had fur, horns, and long tentacles that either came from within its mouth or from its neck. The Snallygaster has a singular large eye on its forehead.

The Snallygaster is unable to approach places protected by a seven-pointed star painted or displayed above the door.

SQUONK

LOCATION: Pennsylvania, United States
CATEGORY: Monster

Squonks are very shy and reclusive animals living in the hemlock forests of Pennsylvania. They are described as hideous and grotesque with skin covered in warts, moles, and acne. In addition, their skin is far too large for their bodies and hangs off them. Squonks know that they are considered ugly and constantly weep because of it. They avoid being seen and hide whenever they can. If a squonk becomes too distressed, it can dissolve into a puddle of its own tears.

Squonks are easy to track, as you only have to follow the sound of their sobbing and the trail of tears. Squonk skin is considered valuable; however, because of their ability to dissolve themselves, they are incredibly difficult to catch.

TIZZIE-WHIZIE

LOCATION: Lake District, England, United Kingdom
CATEGORY: Monster

First spotted in 1900 by a boatsman, the tizzie-whizie is a shy and elusive chimera that skims across the surface of England's Windermere lake. According to the story, in 1906, a panicked tizzie-whizie flew into a photography studio (conveniently) near the lake. It zipped around the room before being calmed with some warm milk and ginger biscuits. Once calm, the tizzie-whizie was photographed before it flew away. The photograph was used on a postcard, which sold thousands of copies in the following decades.

A tizzie-whizie has the body of a hedgehog, the wings of a dragonfly, the antennae of a bee or butterfly, and the tail of a squirrel. It flies and swoops across the surface of the lake and can dive underwater and swim with ease. Tizzie-whizies adore ginger biscuits and warm milk. If you listen near the water, you can hear them squeaking and whistling to each other—just be careful not to lean too close to the water and fall in!

Rachel Q. says: The tizzie-whizie is one of my favorite cryptids! Even if, like the gerota, it is probably a taxidermied abomination, I think it's refreshing to have a peaceful cryptid who enjoys the simple joys of biscuits. There's something very whimsical and almost faerie-like about this cryptid, while being incredibly "British" at the same time.

55

WOLPERTINGER

LOCATION: Germany
CATEGORY: Monster

The wolpertinger is a hybrid of the jackalope (see page 33) and skvader (see page 51). It has the body of a hare (or, in rare cases, a squirrel), the antlers of a deer, the fangs of a canine, and the wings of a grouse or pheasant; some versions give it the hind feet of a duck and the head of a fox. The wolpertinger is far more mischievous than its jackalope cousin but does not tend to be violent or aggressive.

To catch a wolpertinger, you must send a beautiful woman into the woods where the wolpertinger lives. The hybrid will come out to admire the woman. She must expose her breasts to cause the wolpertinger to fall into a trance, allowing it to be simply picked up and bagged by the hunter.

Lyndsey's reimagining of the wolpertinger: A wolpertinger is a creature whose body is made up from several different animals. Most commonly in folklore, it is depicted as a small mammal with the wings, antlers, and tail of other species, but most people do not realize the vast range of wolpertingers that actually exist in the world. Depicted here is the African savanna wolpertinger, which has the body of a serval, the head of a savanna hare, the horns of an oryx, and the wings and feathers of a secretary bird.

The savanna wolpertinger uses its large ears to locate prey in the long grass before jumping high in the air to pounce upon unsuspecting mice, lizards, small birds, and snakes. They have even been known to take flight and drop their prey to its death. The long horns are also a lethal weapon capable of inflicting serious damage, but generally wolpertingers are not threatened by other animals, who seem to keep a wary and respectful distance. It is thought that this may be due to them having otherworldly powers, though they rarely appear to humans, so the full extent of their magic is unconfirmed. They are more in touch with nature than we are, and there are some tales of them being able to control the elements.

FOLKLORE

ASWANG

LOCATION: Philippines

CATEGORY: Humanoid—shapeshifter

CONTENT WARNING: Adult and child death, miscarriage, abortion, and discussion of fetuses

The definition of the aswang varies across the islands of the Philippines and is further complicated as the stories have only been passed down through oral tradition. The belief in aswangs is still prevalent in areas of contemporary society and has been kept alive by grave robberies, missing children, and vanishing corpses. In the past decade, there have been several murders due to individuals believing their loved ones had become aswangs. All versions of aswangs are vampiric in nature and a destructive force of evil. Aswangs are typically believed to appear as women although some sightings have reported aswangs appearing as men. Salt is a common deterrent for aswangs as contact burns their skin. Decapitation is typically considered a guaranteed method of execution.

The most popular version of the aswang describes it appearing in the daytime as a beautiful maiden, able to marry, have children, and live a relatively normal life. At night, however, it becomes a winged, savage monster with a long, narrow tongue that it will use to drain blood. The thin tongue can slip between gaps in a building's structure and puncture its victim before drawing out blood, using its tongue as a straw. Aswangs favor the blood of babies and children. It is advised to put a bowl of salt beside sleeping children to repel the aswang.

An **aswang mandurugo** appears as a beautiful maiden who seeks marriage in order to have a consistent supply of blood. The aswang mandurugo kisses her husband each night and inserts a long, barbed tongue into his mouth and down his throat to drain him of blood. The husband will suffer weight loss and grow weaker as a result but will be unaware that he has married a vampiric beast. If a husband suspects his wife may be an aswang mandurugo, he is advised to sleep with a knife under his pillow in order to strike the vampire in the heart during the next attack. The Tagalog version is slightly different: The aswang mandurugo is a resurrected deceased woman, now possessed by an evil spirit using its magic to keep youthful and fresh.

Aswang manananggal are able to split their bodies at the waist during a full moon. The torso sprouts large, leathery, batlike wings and clawed hands before flying to find its favorite prey: pregnant women. The aswang manananggal prefers to eat by sucking the fetus out of the womb of a pregnant woman using its long tongue. If it is unable to find a fetus, it will settle for human entrails. Pregnant women can avoid this fate by wearing a necklace of bullets and by staining their stomachs with dust and coal. In order to destroy this version of the aswang, you must locate the lower half of the torso while in its divided state and cover it in salt. Upon returning, the torso half will be unable to reattach itself and consequently dies when the sun rises. In order to reproduce more aswang manananggals, it must trick a woman into drinking boiled human blood, upon which the woman transforms into an aswang.

The **aswang shapeshifter** can change into any form it desires, from human to animal and even inanimate objects. Aswang shapeshifters are created by sorcerers who may even transform themselves into the creature. The shapeshifter selects its prey and paralyzes them with a foul odor before creating a duplicate of the victim from banana tree trunks, banana leaves, sticks, and grass. It enchants

the doppelgänger, who appears human and dies shortly after from an unexplained disease. The existence and death of the doppelgänger results in no one searching for or rescuing the human victim. Meanwhile, the original human is captured by the aswang and suffers a long, torturous death. In order to identify that the doppelgänger is a duplicate, your reflection will be upside down if you look into its eyes. Another way to detect this aswang involves brewing a complicated oil that will boil in the presence of an aswang. This oil can only be made on Good Friday—thus lending evidence of colonial Christian influence on the local folklore.

The **aswang tanggal** has spread beyond the borders of the Philippines to countries such as Indonesia, Cambodia, and Malaysia. The aswang tanggal appears as a beautiful woman by day but by night detaches its head and flies by, flapping its intestines, lungs, and ears, hunting for human blood and feces. This aswang can be deterred with garlic, spices, and herbs.

The **aswang tiktik, also known as the aswang wakwak,** is onomatopoeic in nature, as when the beast flies, it makes a tiktik or wakwak sound with its wings. The sound of the tiktik or wakwak indicates how close the creature is. Perversely, if the aswang is far away, the beats will be loud, but if it is close and ready to strike, it will sound distant and quiet. The sound it produces when it flies has led to extensive hunting of Tasmanian devils and Philippine flying lemurs, which are mistaken as aswangs in disguise as they make similar noises. The aswang tiktik is described as having more

birdlike features, and its tongue has a single barb on the end to puncture its victims.

Aswang tiyanaks have multiple origins. One describes them as a vampiric crossbreed between a demon and a human; another says that they are created when a child dies before baptism, and yet another states that they come to life from an aborted fetus. All versions depict the aswang tiyanak as a hairless, ugly child with red skin and glowing eyes who brings misery upon its mother. After killing its mother, it can change its appearance to look cute in order to be "rescued" by another family. Once the family is sleeping, it reveals its true form and drains them of their blood.

The **aswang witch** is a popular version of the aswang due to the historical and cultural fear of witches. They seduce men, lure them home, drink their blood, and eat their innards. Despite this easy prey, the aswang witch still prefers to drink the blood of children. Unlike the other aswangs, the witch can be killed the same way as any mortal.

The creation of an aswang has multiple variations. One involves tricking others to drink human blood (such as the aswang manananggal). The most popular story uses a fertilized chicken's egg. Tie the egg to your stomach, and the chick will pass out of the egg, through your skin, and into your stomach. The empty eggshell is buried in a bamboo tube with coconut oil and chicken dung, and congratulations, you're now an aswang. You may pass on the vampiric gifts by opening your mouth over someone else's, and the chick will hop into the other person's mouth and down into the stomach, thus creating a new aswang. The original host dies and is no longer an aswang.

While most outside (and most within) the Philippines believe the aswang to be part of mythology or a cautionary tale to curb children's bad behavior, some living in rural areas of the Philippines still consider it to be a real and present threat. Local artist Malonzo believes that continued belief in the aswang stems from an intrinsic desire to establish a "collective identity as Filipinos" and hold on to something that is truly "theirs." It is possible that creatures like the aswang were historically used to explain the unexplainable cruelties of life, such as disease, unexplained deaths, and poor crops.

BEAN NIGHE

LOCATION: Scotland, United Kingdom
CATEGORY: Spirit
CONTENT WARNING: Death

The bean nighe is a type of ban-sìth, more popularly known by the Irish variant, a banshee. She is an omen of death found in isolated rivers, singing to herself in Gaelic and washing the bloodstained clothes of those who are about to die. She does not cause the death but is a warning that death is coming to someone. Bean nighe are the spirits of women who died in childbirth and are destined to haunt streams and rivers until the day they would have died if they had not died prematurely. The bean nighe appear as small old women dressed in green with a hooked nose, a single nostril, one protruding tooth, large, red, webbed feet, and sagging breasts.

The bean nighe are able to grant wishes, but they must first be earned. You must sneak between the bean nighe and the river where she is washing and suckle upon one of her breasts. Tell her you are her foster child and she will grant a wish (some versions say she will give you three wishes).

BOO HAG

LOCATION: South Carolina (Gullah regions), United States
CATEGORY: Humanoid
CONTENT WARNING: Death

The Gullah people along the coast of South Carolina tell the story that humans have a spirit and a soul; when you die, if your spirit is good, your soul ascends to Heaven, but if your spirit is evil, you are trapped on Earth as a boo hag. Boo hags are ugly creatures. Once their original skin has rotted away, they are left without flesh and appear bright red with bulging blue veins. They will steal skin from their victims in order to pass as human in society. However, this skin will eventually rot, meaning they must constantly find new skin in order to keep their true form hidden.

Boo hags, similar to aswangs (see page 60), can slither into your house through the smallest crack in the dead of night. Boo hags creep over their sleeping victims, crouch or sit on their chests, and suck out the air from their lungs, often resulting in people waking up feeling tired or poorly rested, which is the most common symptom of a boo hag visit. However, encounters with a boo hag can be deadly: Some sources state that a boo hag will only kill by accident, whereas others state that if you wake up and struggle against a boo hag, she will kill you by sucking out all the air and suffocating you.

Sources vary on how to stop a boo hag from stealing your breath and energy. The most popular story states that you must leave a straw broom by your bed, as the boo hag will be compelled to count every strand of straw and will not have enough time to steal your breath before the sun rises. Boo hags may also be repelled by painting window frames, doors, or the porch of your house indigo blue. Colors are incredibly important in Gullah culture, and indigo blue is associated with the supernatural and warding off evil creatures and witches.

BUNYIP

LOCATION: Australia
CATEGORY: Monster

The bunyip stems from Australian Aboriginal folklore. Stories have been passed on orally for generations, which has resulted in different descriptions of bunyip appearances depending on the storyteller. It is widely accepted that the bunyip lurks underwater in swamps, rivers, billabongs, and watering holes, waiting for prey (humans and live-stock) to roam too close. It favors the sweet taste of women or children. The bunyip's favored method of executing its prey is to hug it, thus crushing it to death. When Europeans began to colonize Australia, they began to write down the tales of the bunyip. It is important therefore to consider how colonization will have colored, redesigned, and resurrected the creature beyond its original stories. Some tales of the bunyip describe it as a bloodthirsty monster, whereas others describe it as a vigilante, punishing evil-doers. In modern times, the bunyip is seen by some as a more wholesome and friendly folklore tale, appearing in children's TV and books.

The descriptions of the bunyip's appearance are broad and colorful. The bunyip has been described as:

- A giant, man-eating starfish
- A snake with a beard
- A crocodile covered with eyes, with large flippers, a horse's tail, a serrated beak, and walrus tusks
- A dark-furred beast, with a dog face, a crocodile head, a duck's bill, and long crocodile legs (with the forelegs longer than the hind legs)
- An emu with large claws
- A humanoid with one large eye, feathers, fur, and a mouth across its stomach.

Across all descriptions, it is generally accepted that the bunyip is very large.

BUSCHGROSSMUTTER ⊛

LOCATION: Germany
CATEGORY: Spirit

Queen of the Moss people, the Buschgroßmutter (Buschgrossmutter) is an ambivalent figure from Germanic fairy tales. Her name translates to "shrub grandmother," but she has also gone by the names of Pusch-Grohla ("shrub granny") or Buschweibchen ("shrub woman"). Usually an isolated figure, she only appears to humans once every hundred years. The Moss matriarch is said to be "as old as the hills" with long white hair that teems with lice. She is a short figure with piercing eyes and feet covered with moss. Some interpretations of the Buschgroßmutter describe her as having an iron head, which is typically seen in demonic characters.

Her nature is difficult to define; she can be both generous and cruel, depending on the encounter. Upon meeting her, she may ask you to comb or remove the lice from her hair, which is far more difficult than anticipated, as her head and hair are bitterly cold, causing the helper's hands to freeze. If you are successful, she may bless you with an unending ball of yarn or yellow leaves that may turn to gold if they are not discarded. If you sneer at or mock her, she will breathe on you and curse you with an illness—most commonly a rash. Other stories speak of her as a malevolent figure, attacking children who are picking berries or stealing milk from cows. She is commonly used as a "bogeyman" figure in certain regions.

According to some narratives, the Buschgroßmutter has several daughters (who are Moss people, like her) who travel with her in a cart or wagon through the forest, but only on holy nights. In other stories, she surrounds herself with creatures such as dwarves, brownies, pixies, and hobgoblins, who attend to her instead of her daughters. Natural phenomena used to be attributed to the Buschgroßmutter; for example, people believed that when fog descended down the mountains, it was because she was cooking, and the fog was the smoke from her cooking pot.

Interestingly, during the 1800s, mythologists believed Busch-großmutter to be a goddess, rivaling the power and abilities of Frau Holle[5] and Perchta.[6] But by the 1900s, Buschgroßmutter's brief promotion to goddess was stripped away, leaving her to be a mere forest demon.

CAT SÍDHE

LOCATION: Ireland, and Scotland, United Kingdom
CATEGORY: Spirit—fae
CONTENT WARNING: Death

Cat sídhe is the Irish name of this creature, which translates to "fairy cat," while in Scotland, it is called cat sìth. Cat sídhes are described as being black cats with a white spot or crest on their chest and are said to be the size of a large dog.

Cat sídhes have an interesting collection of stories behind them. Many believe them to be witches who have transformed into cats. Limited to transforming only eight times between human and cat, on the ninth transformation, the witch would be unable to return to their human form and would be thus trapped as a cat. Some believe this to be the origin of the tale that cats have nine lives. Cat sídhes also appear in the folktale "The King of Cats."[7]

Considered harmless to the living, a cat sídhe is believed to be a great danger to the souls of the recent dead. If a cat sídhe hops over the body of a corpse before it is buried, it steals the soul and prevents it from traveling on to the afterlife. Because of this, when a body was being prepared for burial, people would work together to watch over the body and distract the cat sídhes. Distractions included enticing them away with catnip, playing games of leaping or wrestling (as cat sídhes enjoy watching and participating), playing musical laments for the cat sídhe to dance to, or giving the cat sídhe an unsolvable riddle to ponder over. An additional precaution would be to light a fire in every other room of the house except for where the body was stored, as cat sídhes prefer warm rooms.

On the festival of Samhain (October 31 to November 1), it was customary to leave a plate of milk outdoors for the cat sídhes in order to receive their blessing. Failing to do this could result in the feline fairy cursing your cows to stop them producing milk.

In Scotland, it is believed the cat sìth was inspired by the Kellas cat, a hybrid between a domestic and wild cat. It was believed to be either a hoax or a mythological cat until one was caught in 1984.

La says: Cat sídhe is a creature that in many ways sums up cats exactly—a king to some, untrustworthy to others, and capable of stealing souls, which, as any cat owner knows, is basically any other Tuesday with your feline friends. Whether a witch or a fairy, the cat sídhe is a magical creature and one that has captured my mind for ages. Just make sure to leave out some milk and to always have some catnip to distract your local cat sídhe so that you don't lose your soul and so that your cows always produce milk.

CÙ SÌTH

LOCATION: Scotland, United Kingdom
CATEGORY: Spirit—fae
CONTENT WARNING: Death

Cù sìth translates to "fairy dog," as does the Irish counterpart, cú sídhe. Both share similarities with the Welsh Cŵn Annwn.[8] There is noticeable overlap with other hound folklore of the British Isles, such as the barghest, Black Shuck, church grims, Gytrash, and the gwyllgi, all omens of death. Cù sìth are large, bull-sized hounds with paws as wide as a man's hand, and they have long, shaggy fur that is either green (associated with fairies) or white. Their long tails are traditionally coiled or plaited. The Irish cú sídhe is described as black with glowing red eyes.

Cù sìth are harbingers of death, sharing a similar role to the bean nighe (see page 65) and banshee in Irish folklore. People feared the bark of the cù sìth. The unearthly hound could bark three times at such a volume that it was heard from miles around, even across the ocean. The first bark was a warning showing the hound was on your scent, and the second warned of your limited time, as it was advised to hide indoors if you heard the dog's bark. Those who heard the third bark would be overcome with fear and die of fright. Another story describes the barks as a cautionary tale for men to lock up their wives or else the cù sìth would steal them away. The wives would be taken to a fairy mound, where they would be milked to feed the *daoine sìth* ("fairy folk"). Despite their sinister nature and frightening barks, it is believed that the cù sìth guide souls of the dead to the afterlife.

As a fairy creature, a cù sìth would fear iron and salt—iron nullifies their magic, and they hate the taste of salt.

DOBHAR-CHÚ

LOCATION: Ireland
CATEGORY: Monster

Known as the "Irish Hound of the Deep," the dobhar-chú resides in lakes and streams in Ireland. It is said to be 7 feet (2 meters) long and resembles an otter (sometimes given additional doglike qualities), with a white belly and black tipped ears. There are a few accounts where it is described as half wolf, half fish. It has been nicknamed "the Irish Crocodile" as it can lunge from the water at great speed.

The dobhar-chú has shifted from folklore to cryptid, according to some, after being compared to the Loch Ness Monster (see page 37). However, while the Loch Ness Monster is peaceful and calm, the dobhar-chú is a bloodthirsty beast. Many accounts report a single dobhar-chú attacking; however, a dobhar-chú always travels with its mate and will only reveal itself and attack to get revenge if its mate is killed. When a dobhar-chú is killed, it releases a loud, shrill whistling noise to warn or alert its mate.

Theories have linked the prehistoric *Siamogale melilutra*, the ancestor of the modern-day otter, to the dobhar-chú. *Siamogale melilutra* are the size of a wolf, with incredibly strong jaws that could crush larger prey than the prey of modern-day otters. Perhaps the dobhar-chú story was created after discovering these prehistoric bones, or perhaps prehistoric beasts are still hiding in the dark waters of Ireland.

GRIMALKIN

LOCATION: United Kingdom
CATEGORY: Monster—fae

Often associated with the cat sídhe, grimalkins are feline familiars of witches. Since medieval times, familiars have been believed to be supernatural servants or assistants of witches and could take any form they desired (though it seems a cat was always the favored form).

The name "grimalkin" derives from a nickname for "Maud" or "Matilda" ("malkin") and the color gray. "Malkin" was a name associated with women in poverty or those of a lower social class, with pieces of literature referring to them as "Kitchen Malkins." Malkyne referred to kitchen rags or a mop, furthering the association with women in servitude. The word "grimalkin" later evolved to mean "cat" and "an ill-tempered old woman," only furthering the association with cats and the negative stereotyping of witches.

Multiple sources cite that Shakespeare (1564 to 1616) was the one to invent the term "Graymalkin," which later became "grimalkin" in his play *Macbeth* (1606). Graymalkin is a familiar of one of the three witches and takes the form of a cat. That said, Nostradamus (1503 to 1566) had a cat called Grimalkin, and he died fifty years before the first performance of *Macbeth*. The name was further associated with the supernatural after the playwright Thomas Middleton, in his play *The Witch* (c. 1613 to 1616), named an evil spirit "Malkin," who took the form of a cat.

HAWAIIAN NIGHT MARCHERS

LOCATION: Hawaii, United States
CATEGORY: Spirit

The Hawaiian night marchers, or the Huaka'iPō, are ghostly warriors who rise up and march during nights surrounding the new moon (various sources claim they rise before or after the new moon and on blood moons or red moons). The night marchers march toward ancient battlegrounds, sometimes escorting and guarding gods, goddesses, or revered chiefs in their procession.

The night marchers are typically heard before they are seen, drumming a marching beat on war drums, blowing on conch shells—these sounds are a warning to mortals to leave the area. The odor of death follows soon after, and then the flaming torches light up the night as they approach. The night marchers appear human, dressed in historical battle clothing.

Any mortal who looks upon the night marchers is believed to face a horrific and violent death. Death can only be avoided if you either lie face down before them and do not move as a sign of respect and fear, or if you have an ancestor in the procession. The night marchers are not malicious or cruel with their intentions, marching at night to try and avoid being seen. To deter the night marchers from approaching your home, it is advised to grow *ti* plants in your garden, as the night marchers will detour to avoid your house. In addition, *ti* plants will ward off evil spirits.

HERNE THE HUNTER ⭐

LOCATION: Windsor, England, United Kingdom
CATEGORY: Spirit
CONTENT WARNING: Animal death

Evidence of Herne the Hunter, or the Greenman, can be traced back to Shakespeare's play *The Merry Wives of Windsor*; however, many academics believe the origin of the story to be much older. Some theorize him to be a localized symbol or leader of the Wild Hunt.[9] His originating story has various embellishments but consistently ends in Herne hanging himself from an oak tree (later named Herne's Oak). Nowadays, Herne is believed to haunt Windsor Forest, tormenting cattle, rattling ghostly chains, and leading the hunt on the night of the Wild Hunt, but rarely will he appear to mortal men. Herne rides a great black horse, has deerlike antlers, and carries a horn or wooden bow.

Some scholars believe he may have been inspired by tales of Odin, as Windsor was populated by Anglo-Saxons and one of Odin's titles was "Herian."

Morrighan says: I've always been fascinated with forest spirits—it's interesting how they change from place to place while still retaining a strange similarity among them all. I particularly like Herne the Hunter because nobody can work out whether he's a Shakespearean work of fiction, a lost deity figure, or a real person who died so awfully that his story passed into local legend. Not knowing why this terrible spirit roams through Windsor Forest makes it all the more mysterious and enthralling.

KELPIE

LOCATION: Scotland, United Kingdom
CATEGORY: Spirit—shapeshifter
CONTENT WARNING: Death

The shapeshifting kelpies typically take the form of large black horses who linger by the edges of bodies of water. If you approach a kelpie and stroke or try to ride it, you will become stuck to the horse, and it will drag you into the water and drown you. A common folktale tells of a kelpie capturing nine brothers upon its back while the tenth escaped. The kelpie chased down the tenth brother until he touched the kelpie's nose, becoming stuck. With that, the kelpie began to drag the boys away, but the tenth brother cut off his finger and escaped. He survived, while his nine brothers were drowned by the beast.

Kelpies may appear as beautiful human women, luring men into the water to drown them—a popular theme in mythology and folklore. The arrival of Christianity in Scotland changed the narrative: The human depiction of the spirit was unable to hide her hoofed feet, which resulted with kelpies being linked to the Devil.

To tame a kelpie, you must acquire a kelpie's bridle, as it will give authority over any kelpie you see. Kelpies are physically ten times stronger than horses, so owning a kelpie's bridle has plenty of advantages. Kelpies can be killed with a silver bullet (the same as a werewolf), and after the arrival of Christianity, it was believed you could exorcize a kelpie spirit.

Kelpies were used as cautionary tales to young children to keep them away from dangerous bodies of water. The majority of kelpie stories focus on Loch Ness; however, every loch in Scotland has its own kelpie story.

Fun fact: As a kelpie enters the water, its tail slaps against the surface and sounds like thunder.

Rachel says: Scottish mythology has always been so interesting to me, and I love to speculate the reasons for the stories surrounding these beasts. A friend of mine once said that, when he was younger, his dad used to warn him and his brother not to go near open water because the kelpie would get them. His brother was so afraid that he refused to take baths!

MAPINGUARI

LOCATION: Brazil and later the rest of South America
CATEGORY: Monster

The mapinguari's name translates literally to "the roaring animal" or "the fetid beast," though many non-natives refer to the creature as the "Bigfoot of the Amazon." It stands at an impressive 6 feet, 6 inches (2 meters) tall. The mapinguari is an aggressive creature, hunting down those who transgress, take more than their share of meat and flora from the forest, or hunters who use exceptionally cruel traps.

Several sightings describe the mapinguari to be a humanoid with large claws that can slice through trees and to have a large mouth across its stomach to devour humans who are too slow to escape. Its feet face backward, throwing potential trackers off its path. It oozes a vile, putrid scent of rotting meat. Sources disagree on whether the beast has two eyes or a singular cyclopean eye. In addition, some describe this version of the mapinguari to have either scalelike skin or matted reddish-brown fur.

Others describe the mapinguari to resemble a large bear with sloth claws. This version shares the horrific stench and sometimes has the distinct stomach-mouth. Because of the description of the bear with sloth claws, it has stirred up speculation as to whether it could be a surviving *Megatherium*, a giant land sloth from thousands of years ago. However, fossil evidence suggests that these creatures have been extinct for over twelve thousand years.

SEA MONK/BISHOP FISH

LOCATION: Denmark
CATEGORY: Monster

Sea monks tormented Danish sailors in the 1500s, as an encounter with the fish would bring about a storm strong enough to capsize their boats. Sea monks are aquatic creatures with a domed, human head and a crude and jarring face. They are covered in scales, have two prominent fins, and wear a monk's cowl.

A bishop fish is very similar to the sea monk, but instead of wearing a monk's robe, its head is pointed like a bishop's hat (or like a shark). A bishop fish was caught in the 1500s and begged the king of Poland to release it. Upon being granted its wish, the creature made the sign of the cross and returned to the sea.

Modern scholars theorize that sea monks and bishop fish are actually misidentified angel sharks (contemporarily called monkfish in the United Kingdom) or a species of stingray as both species have vaguely humanoid faces that could be misidentified through the water. Others believe that they may have been seals.

SELKIE

LOCATION: Scotland, United Kingdom
CATEGORY: Humanoid—shapeshifter
CONTENT WARNING: Abuse, child death

Selkies are benevolent creatures that live around the coasts of Scotland, Greenland, and Northern Ireland, though their tale began in the north of Scotland. Typically, they take the form of a gray seal, but they have the ability to remove their skin and take the form of a human. The seal skin, or "selkie coat," is central to selkie folklore, as without the selkie coat, they are trapped in their human forms, which is treated as a miserable existence in selkie stories. There are varying statements on how frequently a selkie may transform; some sources say they can change once a year on Midsummer Eve, some say on every ninth night, while some say they may change at will.

There are several accounts of selkies marrying humans or seeking their company for sexual pleasure before returning to the ocean. Many stories depict female selkies who have been forced into marrying the man who owns their coat. No matter how joyous or happy the selkie is with married life, the moment they find their coat, they flee to the ocean, transform, and disappear beneath the waves. In these stories, the coat is often returned to them by one of their human children who is unaware of the coat's powers. Whether the children remain with the mortal parent or join their selkie parent in the ocean as selkies depends on the storyteller. In more tragic endings, the children who follow the selkie parent into the ocean are unable to transform and subsequently drown.

Selkies are blamed for the disappearance of young women who travel down to the sea in search of a lover. Young women must shed seven tears into the ocean to summon a male selkie. In their human forms, selkies are depicted as being irresistible and gorgeous, regardless of sexual preference.

The animal bride (or partner) trope is not unique to selkies and can be seen across the world. In Europe, swan maidens (who could be any gender, despite their name) would take the form of a swan, and to bathe, they remove a robe of swan feathers to take the form of a human. If the robe is stolen, they are forced to marry the thief and have their children. The children return the robe to the swan maiden, who transforms back into a swan and leaves forever. In Croatia, there is the same narrative with a she-wolf; in Italy, it is a dove maiden instead of a swan, and in Africa, a buffalo maiden.

SHELLYCOAT

LOCATION: Scotland, United Kingdom
CATEGORY: Humanoid

Traditionally depicted as one of Scotland's bogeymen, shellycoats lurk in water, waiting for humans to play tricks on. Typically found in rivers, shellycoats mimic the sound of a drowning human and laugh as a human becomes distracted and searches for the drowning man. On occasion, they will make sounds to mislead humans who wander into their territory. Despite their mischievous ways, shellycoats are not malicious and rarely cause physical harm to humans.

Shellycoats are depicted as ugly humanoids, covered in shells that rattle as they move. Some shellycoats appear in human clothing, resembling hags more than monsters, while in other interpretations they resemble goblins or trolls.

SHUG MONKEY

LOCATION: Cambridge, England, United Kingdom
CATEGORY: Spirit

The Shug Monkey haunts Slough Hill Lane in Cambridgeshire, England. It is considered a ghost or demonic entity with the body of a large shaggy sheepdog, black fur, and the face of a monkey. The Shug Monkey moves on all fours, leaving a bizarre footprint shaped like a dog's print but with long, flattened claws protruding from it like human fingernails.

The Shug Monkey is often associated with werewolf legends due to its canine features. However, it has more in common with the British Black Shuck, a spectral black hound who stalks the lands and churchyards of East Anglia (Cambridge, Norfolk, Suffolk, and Essex). The Black Shuck is traditionally seen as an omen of death, similar to the cù sìth (see page 75). There have been no official sightings of the Shug Monkey since World War II.

TAILYPO ⭐

LOCATION: Appalachia, United States
CATEGORY: Monster
CONTENT WARNING: Death, animal death

The stories of the Tailypo typically describe a starving hunter and his dogs returning after an unsuccessful hunt with only a measly rabbit to feed all four of them. On his return to his hut, the hunter sees a strange shape with bright eyes and a thick, bushy tail. Fueled by hunger, he shoots the creature, severing its tail from its body. The creature wails and flees into the darkness of the forest. The hunter takes the tail and feeds the rabbit to his dogs while eating the tail himself.

That night, there is a loud scratching on the walls of his cabin, and the distant whisper of *"tailypo, tailypo, give me back my tailypo!"* He sends his three dogs out to investigate the creature, but only two dogs return. Later in the night, the scratching sound returns, but this time on the door of his cabin. The voice is louder now: *"Tailypo, tailypo, I want my tailypo!"* He sends out the two hounds to chase away the beast, but only one dog returns. Night progresses on, and the clawing sound echoes from within his cabin. *"Tailypo! Tailypo! Give me back my tailypo!"* The man sends his last hound to chase away the beast, but it does not return.

Alone, the man cowers in his cabin as the scratching noise grows louder and louder. A figure appears at the end of his bed, covered in dark fur, with two long ears and clawed hands.

"Tailypo, tailypo! I want my tailypo!" it snarls.

"I don't have your tailypo!" the man cries. "I ate it!"

The beast leaps onto the man's chest, pinning him down as it hisses, *"You've got my tailypo."*

By morning, the only trace left of the hunter is his torn, blood-soaked clothing. If you listen closely to the morning breeze, you can hear the distant whispering of *"tailypo, tailypo, I've got my tailypo."*

The Tailypo is a popular urban legend told around campfires. Some variations name the dogs and state whether they fled into the forest or were killed by the Tailypo. Another story that mirrors the Tailypo narrative is called "The Devil's Big Toe," in which a woman digs up a big toe along with her potatoes and eats it, only for a demon to appear to her in the night and demand its toe back.

TATZELWURM

LOCATION: The Alps, Europe
CATEGORY: Monster
CONTENT WARNING: Death

Depending on which part of the Alps you visit, tatzelwurms have different names. In France, they are called *arassas*, in Switzerland they are called either *tatzelwurms* or *bergstutzen*, and Slovenians refer to the species as *daazelwurms* or *hockwurms*. In Austria, they are named *lindwurms*, *praatzelwurms*, or *tatzelwurms*, and the latter name is also used in Bavaria in Germany. Despite the many different names, tatzelwurms are just one species of many European dragons.

Tatzelwurm stories state that the creatures can vary between 2 and 6 feet (60 and 183 centimeters) long. They have the body of a snake with two front legs (often clawed) and either the head and face of a cat or a snake face with feline features. They are usually white or pale pink and covered in very fine, smooth scales that they lick to keep clean. Some tatzelwurm reports state that the creatures may have four legs, but the hind legs are usually too stubby to be of use. One account states that tatzelwurms have multiple legs like a caterpillar, while other reports state that they have no legs at all.

Tatzelwurms have multiple ways to protect themselves. They can coil their bodies and spring out of danger (or launch themselves at their prey), and they have the agility of lizards. Their skin is thick enough to not be harmed by a hunting knife, and they can spray a poisonous gas from their mouth. Their blood is believed to be highly acidic and is bright green in color. One story documents a hunter who was successful in killing a tatzelwurm and raised his sword above his head in victory; however, blood from the wurm dripped from his sword and touched his skin, killing him instantly.

Tatzelwurms live in burrows underground and are typically nocturnal creatures who hibernate for most of the year. Tatzelwurm burrows are usually identified by finding the shedded skin of a maturing tatzelwurm. They do not hunt humans, preferring to find farms with cows, and drink milk directly from the cow's udders.

Farmers would leave white roosters near their cows, as tatzelwurms would be too frightened to approach.

Skeptics theorize that the tatzelwurm may be a misidentified species of salamander, Gila monster, or otter.

VAMPIRE PUMPKIN/ WATERMELON

LOCATION: Balkan Peninsula, Europe
CATEGORY: Flora

According to Romani and Slavic folk legends, pumpkins and watermelons are the only two types of vegetation that may become vampiric in nature. If a pumpkin or watermelon is left out under a full moon or kept for ten days after Christmas, it will turn into a vampire. Once transformed, the pumpkin or watermelon will roll around and pester the living with snarls or by knocking into furniture. A vampire pumpkin or watermelon can be identified by spots of blood appearing on the flesh of the fruit.

Vampiric food is not feared, as even though they will try to bite, they do not have any teeth. They can still be a menace, so the best way to remove them is to place the vampire pumpkin or watermelon in a pot of boiling water, scrub them with a broom, and then burn the broom.

WILL-O'-THE-WISP

LOCATION: Worldwide
CATEGORY: Fae
CONTENT WARNING: Death

Lights dancing in the distance may seem like a welcoming sight, but be warned, will-o'-the-wisps are mischievous creatures who lure travelers out into dangerous locations or leave them stranded and lost in the wilderness. In the United Kingdom, will-o'-the-wisps are named after a man named Will or Jack (jack-of-the-lantern is another name for the creatures) who is cursed to haunt swamps and forests for his misdeeds, luring his victims into the dangerous marshes.

In Ireland, the protagonist of the tale tricks the Devil three times, his life extending with each trick; however, when he finally dies and goes to Hell, the Devil rejects him, forcing his spirit to linger on Earth as a will-o'-the-wisp.

Several cultures and countries have their own tales and versions of the will-o'-the-wisp. In Mexico, will-o'-the-wisps are referred to as treasure lights, as following the lights with the aid of a child can lead to treasure. The lights may also be witches who are traveling. In Argentina, the color of the wisp can signify whether a soul is in need of prayer (white) or if the Devil himself has come to find a victim (red). Bengali wisps are believed to be the lost souls of fishermen who lure other fishermen to their deaths. In the Republic of Trinidad and Tobago, they are called soucouyants. These are witches who travel as flaming orbs at night and creep into homes through any gaps they can find to drink the blood of those who are sleeping, reminiscent of the aswang (see page 60).

For centuries, people theorized that will-o'-the-wisps were fireflies or light reflecting off a barn owl. In the 1700s, after the discovery of methane, it was theorized that will-o'-the-wisps were actually balls of methane gas released from swamps that were struck by lightning, causing them to catch on fire. Modern scientists generally agree will-o'-the-wisps are a result of gaseous compounds released from decaying life forms. The gas contains chemicals that ignite when

exposed to oxygen, creating the dancing-light effect. That said, this does not explain why will-o'-the-wisps retreat when approached.

Another interesting scientific explanation for will-o'-the-wisps is the weather phenomenon of St. Elmo's fire, which only occurs during thunderstorms. St. Elmo's fire manifests as a blue flame, typically at the tip of a boat mast, church steeples, or similarly tall, pointed objects that act as lightning rods. (It has been seen on blades of grass, leaves, and cattle horns). The phenomenon is caused by a strong electric field that begins to glow blue or violet due to the oxygen and nitrogen in the air.

WULVER ★

LOCATION: Shetland Islands, Scotland, United Kingdom
CATEGORY: Humanoid

The Wulver is often labeled a werewolf; however, according to Celtic beliefs, the Wulver evolved from wolves to become humanoid and should be considered a species of his own. He lived in a cave carved out of stone on the side of a steep hill. The Wulver spent his days sitting on his favorite rock (now named "Wulver's Stane" or "Wolf Stone") while fishing. In some stories, the Wulver would leave the excess fish he caught on the windowsills of less-fortunate families during the night. He would give directions to lost travelers, sometimes even escorting them home safely. That said, the Wulver preferred solitude, enjoying a peaceful and calm existence.

Skeptics theorize that the Wulver may have been a human with hypertrichosis, or "werewolf syndrome," a condition that causes an excess growth of hair all over the body.

Cory says: I've long admired benevolent cryptids. While many fantastical creatures are very neat, they often come coupled with scary stories about their vicious natures. Creatures like the Wulver I feel are truer to their animal inspirations—not bloodthirsty killers but just creatures of this world that would rather be left in peace and quiet.

YA-TE-VEO AND CARNIVOROUS FLORA

CATEGORY: Plant
CONTENT WARNING: Death, human sacrifice

Carnivorous trees that threaten human life are stories that are told all across the world and rose to fame during the 1880s as Europeans colonized and spread out into unexplored territories.

In 1955, it was decided by Willy Ley that all the stories outlined were mere fabrications conjured up by the allure of exploration and colonialism in order to sensationalize and make money. There is a theory that the idea of man-eating plants was created upon discovery of the corpse flower, a plant that can grow up to 9 feet (2.7 meters) tall and releases a vile, pungent odor, said to smell like rotting flesh and excrement. The corpse flower matches a story by William Wescott Fink, who wrote *Echoes from Erin* (1903) about the fictitious logbook of Captain Arkwright, who claimed to have discovered an island in the Pacific Ocean called El-Banoor, or the Island of Death. He describes in his logs a great hooded flower that gave off a sedative perfume, causing the human to fall asleep before being enveloped and devoured by the flower. This concept is not entirely fictional: *Amorphophallus* uses the smell of rotting meat to trick beetles and flies into thinking there is a rotting corpse for them to lay their eggs in. When the eggs hatch, the insects work as pollinators for the plant.

YA-TE-VEO ⭐
LOCATION: Madagascar

One of the most popular narratives of the Ya-te-veo from Central America and Africa states that the tree is named after the hissing noise it makes. Spookily, *ya-te-veo* translates to "I see you." The tree has long tendrils covered in thick spikes that can individually articulate with the dexterity of an octopus. The tendrils lie in wait for approaching prey, snatching it up in a barbed vine and crushing the blood from its victim before absorbing it through its roots. This description matches accounts of the Arbor Diaboli, the Devil Tree of Mexico, from 1890.

DEVIL'S SNARE ⭐

LOCATION: Nicaragua

In Nicaragua there are tales of the Vampire Vine, or Devil's Snare. It is described less like a tree and more like a series of low vines that weave out from swamps to snatch their prey. It is black and oozes a dark, sticky gum to slow attempts to escape, while the tendrils themselves are covered in multiple mouths.

JUBOKKO ⭐

LOCATION: Japan

Finally, the jubokko is a yokai (a creature from Japanese folklore) that appears on battlefields where many individuals have died, and it appears as an ordinary tree. At first, a jubokko will drink the blood from the dead until it has drained all the corpses on the battlefield. Afterward, it waits for people to pass by before transforming one of its branches into a long tube to drink their blood. Apparently, the branch of a jubokko can heal any injury, and instead of sap, the tree leaks blood when cut.

MAN-EATING TREE OF MINDANAO ⭐

LOCATION: Philippines

In 1920, the *American Weekly* published a story describing the Man-Eating Tree of Mindanao in the Philippines. It had a squat trunk textured like a pineapple and eight leaves—reported to be 10 to 12 feet (3 to 3.6 meters) long—that each tapered down into a sharp needle. In the center of the leaves was a large pool of nectar of which even a small quantity could place a human into a coma. Beneath the leaves, there were six palpi (appendages that surround the mouths of certain insects). In the story, a girl is sacrificed to the tree, and depending on the mood of the devil inside of the tree, she would live or die. It goes on to document how she is held in place by the palpi before being crushed by the eight leaves that raised up and closed around her like a press before digesting her.

MYTHOLOGY

ABADA

LOCATION: Democratic Republic of the Congo
CATEGORY: Monster

The Abada is a shy herbivore from central Africa that shares many similarities with the European mythical creature of the unicorn (see page 162). An Abada is described as having the body and frame of a donkey, standing between 3 to 5 feet (1 to 1.5 meters) tall with a boar-like tail and, in contrast to unicorns, two large, crooked horns. These horns are believed to be an antidote to all poisons.

The Abada also goes by the names of Nillekma and Arase. The beast has physical similarities with the Sudanese A'nasa.

AL-MI'RAJ

LOCATION: Qazvin, Iran
CATEGORY: Monster
CONTENT WARNING: Animal death and disease

The al-mi'raj is found in Islamic mythology and ancient Arabic poetry, with its first appearance in *Marvels of Things Created and Miraculous Aspects of Things Existing* by Zakariya al-Qazwini in 1206. The creature lives on a mythical island called Jezîrat al-Tennyn ("Sea-Serpent Island") in the Indian Ocean. It is unlikely to strike fear into the hearts of the ill-informed, who may judge it as a child's dream of a unicorn (see page 162) and rabbit hybrid. The al-mi'raj are reputed to be fantastically dangerous beasts and incredibly territorial and aggressive. Make the error of entering their territory and it is believed that the al-mi'raj will hunt you relentlessly until it stabs you to death with its horn.

Despite only being the size of a rabbit, al-mi'raj is reported to kill and devour prey significantly larger than itself, including livestock and humans. People of the phantom island Jezîrat al-Tennyn so feared al-mi'raj and its insatiable appetite that they sought the aid of witches for protection. It is believed that only a true witch can soothe the fury and hunger of this murderous beast, rendering it temporarily docile and harmless and allowing the locals to move it away from their village.

Much like the jackalope (see page 33), skvader (see page 51), and wolpertinger (see page 57), stories of the al-mi'raj are likely to be based on the externally visible symptoms of papillomatosis or fibromatosis viruses, which create "hornlike" protrusions. The viruses are well documented today, and a rabbit infected with the virus would be in considerable pain, which would explain the fierce and aggressive behavior.

AO AO

LOCATION: Paraguay
CATEGORY: Monster
CONTENT WARNING: Sexual assault (in Notes)

The Ao Ao originates from South American mythology. The first Ao Ao was the child of Tau and Kerena.[10] They had seven children, each one cursed to be born as different monsters by the goddess Arasy. Ao Ao was the sixth child, cursed to appear as a monstrous sheep. Since the birth of the first Ao Ao, it has produced multiple offspring, which have spread across the hills and mountains of Paraguay.

Ao Ao are described as gigantic, fanged, sheeplike creatures or, in some interpretations, share similarities to a peccary (a species of pig). Ao Ao are carnivorous beasts, devouring only human meat to satiate their hunger. An Ao Ao will stalk its prey for miles across any terrain, howling "ao ao!" as it hunts. Should the human prey try to escape by climbing up a tree, it will continue to howl, digging up the roots until the tree falls. The only way to escape an Ao Ao is to climb a palm tree, as the roots are too wide for the creature to dig up; the creature will howl in defeat before retreating to find a new victim.

The Ao Ao is used to threaten children into good behavior, similar to the Chupacabra (see page 8) and the bogeyman.

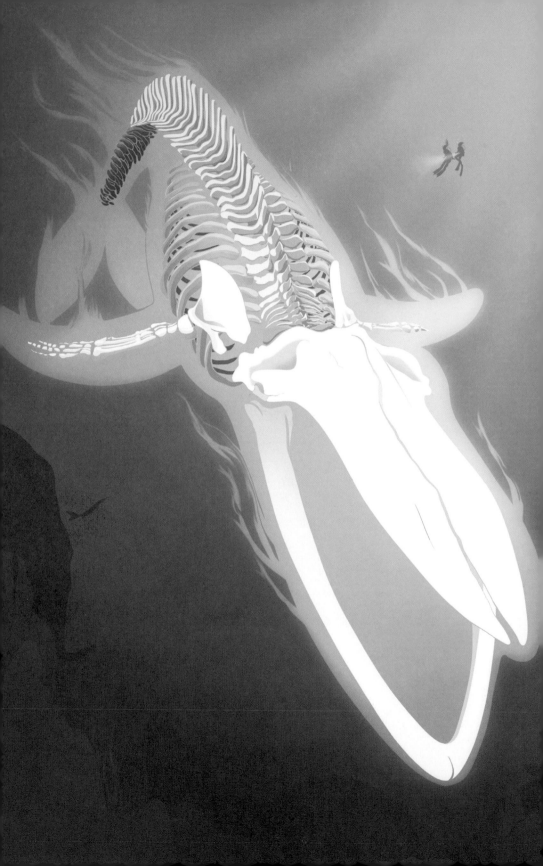

BAKE-KUJIRA ★

LOCATION: Japan
CATEGORY: Spirit—yokai
CONTENT WARNING: Death

The Bake-kujira belongs to the bakemono class of yokai. The word *bakemono* translates to "a thing that changes," and the class includes beings that could be considered "ghosts" or horrific abominations. The sea-dwelling Bake-kujira is not a shapeshifting creature; it appears as a giant, spectral whale skeleton. Bake-kujira is usually accompanied by ghoulish-looking birds and fish. It is a harbinger of bad fortune, and those who see it are blighted with a horrific curse. The curse brings famine, fires, plagues, and a multitude of disasters to their entire village.

When first sighted, the Bake-kujira was mistaken for a white whale, and a fisherman threw his harpoon at the beast. The harpoon missed the Bake-kujira, traveling between its bones and down into the depths. The fisherman saw gruesome fish writhing over the surface of the ocean, and strange birds filled the skies. In the distance, a mysterious island suddenly appeared. Then, just as quickly as the Bake-kujira had appeared, it dived down and disappeared, its nightmarish entourage following in its wake before vanishing.

The Bake-kujira is an interesting creature, as whales were seen as a blessing from the sea because of how much meat and fat a whale could provide for a community. The Bake-kujira is the antithesis of how whales are often represented within Japanese culture.[11]

BIFANG ⭐

LOCATION: China
CATEGORY: Monster

The Bifang, or Bi Fang, is a mythological bird that resembles a crane but has only one leg. Its body is either white or blue depending on the source. Some describe it as having red markings on its face, while others state that the markings are on its back. The Bifang has a long white beak that it can use to carry fire across the land. A Bifang sighting is considered to be a warning of the commencement of a massive wildfire.

The name "Bifang" is supposedly either the onomatopoeic sound of crackling fire or the sound that the bird cries out.

BUKAVAC

LOCATION: East Slovenia
CATEGORY: Monster
CONTENT WARNING: Assault

Bukavacs are demonic monsters from Slavic mythology that reside in lakes and rivers. They have six legs and a pair of gnarled horns. When night falls, bukavacs emerge from the water, making a loud noise (*buka* is Slovenian for "noise") before pouncing on an unsuspecting human or animal and then strangling them to death.

CUÉLEBRE

LOCATION: Asturias, Spain
CATEGORY: Monster

Cuélebre stem from Asturian and Cantabrian mythologies in northern Spain prior to the Roman Empire, which begin invading the Iberian Peninsula in 218 BCE. It is believed that the mythology and beliefs about cuélebre were diluted by Celtic and Roman mythology over the years before being denounced as pagan by the Christian church. Cuélebre are described as large, serpentlike dragons with bat-like wings, eyes that burn like embers, and foul-smelling breath.

They dwell in large caves, guarding stolen treasure and enslaving xanas.[12] They feed on local livestock and sometimes local villagers; in order to avoid this fate, people supply the cuélebre with food to pacify it. Despite eating humans and animals, its favorite food is boroña, a type of cornbread. Cuélebre are (usually) immortal, and as they age, their strong scales become heavier and thicker until they are no longer able to remain on Earth due to their size. When they reach late adulthood, cuélebre will leave for Mar Cuajada, a magical land beneath the ocean, which is guarded by even older cuélebre.

In order to kill a cuélebre and release your village from the burden of feeding the dragon, you can trick it by feeding it a loaf of bread filled with pins or a hot stone hidden in the cornbread (although one tale tells how a cuélebre was quick enough to fly into the sea and cool the stone it had eaten before the stone was able to kill it). In midsummer, between June 19 and June 25, the cuélebre is not protected by magic and is particularly vulnerable. On Midsummer Eve, brave men would travel to kill a cuélebre, marry a xana, and steal the treasure. However, on St. Bartholomew's night (August 24), the cuélebre doubles in strength and may seek revenge on anyone who tried to hunt it during midsummer.

Fun fact: Their saliva is believed to turn into a magical stone with healing properties.

GASHADOKURO

LOCATION: Japan
CATEGORY: Spirit—yokai
CONTENT WARNING: Death and starvation

One of the many yokai that haunt Japan, a gashadokuro is formed from the bones of those who died of starvation on the battlefield and were not buried. Hundreds of bones are required to form a gashadokuro, which stands fifteen times taller than the average human. At midnight, fueled by hunger, malice, and envy of the living, gashadokuro stalk those who are alone on the road, snatch them up, and crush them or bite off their heads before drinking their blood. Despite the gashadokuro's ability to turn invisible, you can hear them approaching by a ringing sound in your ear.

Gashadokuro are believed to be indestructible, but their ability to turn invisible can be neutralized by a Shinto charm. A gashadoruko can be put to rest if the remaining bones of the starved fighters are buried with food. However, a gashadoruko will cease to exist when the malice and energy that once fueled the spirit have dried up. Once the energy has been extinguished, the skeleton collapses.

GROOTSLANG

LOCATION: Richtersveld, South Africa
CATEGORY: Monster
CONTENT WARNING: Death

Grootslang translates to "big snake" in Afrikaans and Dutch; however, that's only half the story. Grootslangs were one of the first creations of the gods who, in their inexperience, blessed the grootslangs with too much strength, intelligence, and cunning. As the grootslangs grew in size and strength, the gods realized their error and divided the chimera like creatures in two, creating the first elephants and the first snakes. One of the original grootslangs, however, escaped the division and still to this day lives in a cave referred to as "the bottomless cave." This cave is believed to be filled with diamonds.

The grootslang covets riches and jewels, similarly to a dragon in Western mythology. It favors diamonds over all other gems. Despite the beast being inherently violent and cruel, if you give it enough gems or diamonds, you will be able to release yourself from its wrath. It is believed that the grootslang still hides in South Africa; it was blamed for the 1917 deaths of Peter Grayson and his team, who traveled to Richtersveld in search of the cave filled with diamonds.

HAFGUFA, KRAKEN, AND LYNGBAKR ⭐

LOCATION: North Sea and Scandinavia
CATEGORY: Monster
CONTENT WARNING: Death

According to Norse mythology, the largest whale in the ocean was called Lyngbakr, and it was so large that it carried an island on its back. It would lure sailors to come ashore on its back before sinking back into the ocean and drowning its victims. In ancient texts from the 1200s, it is described alongside the Hafgufa as a separate creature, though they are very similar to each other.

The Hafgufa is the size of a large island, with a mouth as wide as the Norwegian fjords are deep and teeth that are mistaken for cliffs. Texts from the 1700s describe the Hafgufa to rise up from the ocean, appearing as a small island surrounded by tentacles (or in some versions, trees). Occasionally, the Hafgufa was called "crab-like." As it submerges, it creates a violent whirlpool or undercurrent, dragging down boats that were too close. Despite being such a dangerous force, the beast was believed to be a good omen by fishermen, as large shoals of fish would swim above it. The Hafgufa is believed to be one of the initial names or interpretations of the Kraken.

The popular image of the Kraken as an octopus or squid began in the 1800s, after the giant squid was identified as a species in 1857. From 1870 to 1890, tentacles between 25 and 35 feet long and entire specimens were washed up on the shore of Newfoundland, Canada, and New Zealand. This perpetuated the myth of the Kraken as an octopus or squid. Many people use the names "Kraken" and "Leviathan" interchangeably; however, they are two very different creatures. In addition, the Kraken is often mistaken to be part of Greek mythology, perhaps misinterpreting Scylla or Charybdis as the Kraken, while the Kraken stems from creatures of Norse mythology. The myth of the Kraken being part of Greek mythology was perpetuated through the film *The Clash of the Titans* (1981) and its remake in 2010.

HARPY

LOCATION: Greek
CATEGORY: Humanoid

Known as the "hounds of mighty Zeus," harpies were instruments of the gods used to punish those who were evil or individuals who irritated them. In the *Argonautica*, the Greek epic poem by Apollonius Rhodius, harpies are sent as punishment against King Phineus of Thrace for using his gift of prophecy against the gods. According to the poem, the harpies steal food from the king's hands and either eat it themselves or spoil it. Harpies were believed to kidnap people and take them to the Erinyes[13] as a form of punishment, resulting in harpies being blamed for sudden and unexplained disappearances.

Harpies are presented on pottery as being beautiful women with wings and, in some writings, as fair maidens with lovely hair. In other literature, they are described as ugly beasts with the lower body of a bird and said to have a ravenous hunger. Later reports depict them as monsters of the underworld rather than godly punishments.

LESHY ⊛

LOCATION: Russia and Ukraine
CATEGORY: Spirit—shapeshifter

Leshy is a guardian spirit of the forest, presented as a trickster with a strong set of personal morals. In some texts, he is described as a demon; however, this could be attributed to modern Christianity trying to quash native beliefs and superstitions. Some believe Leshy was the earthly form of the god Veles.[14] Leshy guards the forest, the plants, and the animals within, some of whom serve and aid him in protecting and nurturing the forest. He is assisted in protecting the forest by spirits and ghosts and, in some accounts, demons.

Leshy is a shapeshifter, appearing as tall as the trees while roaming within his forest before shrinking down to the size of a blade of grass once he steps beyond the perimeter. He may take the form of an old man in furs, a humanoid "creature," a cyclops, a bear, all varieties of plants, and even the wind. Many modern depictions present him as a leafy humanoid. If he takes the form of a man, he can be recognized by his missing right ear, missing eyelashes, missing eyebrows, and lack of a belt. It is unlikely that you will see Leshy, but he can be heard in his forest laughing, singing, and whistling.

Leshy is believed to punish those who commit crimes within his forest, including chopping down his trees or hunting an animal from his personal flock. Punishments include ensnaring a criminal in vines, tricking them to get lost within the forest, releasing his flock of animals to attack the perpetrator, or driving the criminal to madness by feeding them poisonous flora. Despite his fierce punishments, it is believed that Leshy enjoys the company of kind humans, especially if they bring him tobacco. For his own entertainment, he may trick humans into taking incorrect paths deeper into his forest. To escape his trickery, humans are advised to remove all their clothes, put them on back to front, and put their shoes on the opposite feet, as this will gain his respect. If that fails, start a forest fire, the old stories say; Leshy will be so concerned with the fire that he will forget you and release you from his spell. Modern interpretations see Leshy as a trickster or similar to the Erl-King,[15] who abducts humans for his own delight.

LEVIATHAN ⍟

LOCATION: Mesopotamia
CATEGORY: Monster

The Leviathan is an ancient sea monster found in the Old Testament of the Bible and Jewish mythology. The Leviathan is a great sea dragon or serpent that is so large that as it rises to the surface, it boils the ocean around it. The beast can breathe fire and has a double layer of scales so thick that harpoons and swords are unable to penetrate. It is over 300 miles (483 kilometers) long.

The Leviathan is a primordial beast, stemming from pre-Biblical Mesopotamian myths (c. 6000 BCE). He ruled the seas with a female mate who was created to keep him company in the ocean; however, it was believed that any offspring they created would devour the earth. Yahweh descended and slew the female Leviathan. The male became bitter and lonely and swore revenge against Yahweh; they are due to reunite in combat at the end of the world. Yahweh will defeat the male Leviathan, and use his beautiful skin as a canopy.

Imagery of the giant sea dwelling beast has passed through multiple mythos. In Norse, it appears as Jörmungandr, a snake so long it can circle the earth and swallow its own tail. It appears as Typhon in Greek mythology, Tiamat in Babylonian mythology, and Lotan in Mesopotamian. "Leviathan" is now synonymous with any large oceanic monster.

MEDUSA ⭐

LOCATION: Greek

CATEGORY: Humanoid

CONTENT WARNING: Death, sexual assault

According to Hesiod's story, Medusa was born a beautiful and mortal Gorgon, unlike her two sisters, Stheno and Euryale, who were born ugly but immortal. All three sisters had snakes for hair.

The alternative and more famous narrative was written by Ovid centuries later. Medusa was a beautiful priestess in Athena's shrine who caught the wandering eye of Poseidon, god of the sea. She rejected his advances but was raped on Athena's altar by the sea god. Furious at the desecration of her altar, Athena punished Medusa by transforming her into a Gorgon, cursing her to turn anyone who looked at her into stone.[16]

Perseus[17] was sent to kill Medusa. He was aided by the gods, who gave him divine objects, including a shield with a mirrored surface from Athena, used to allow Perseus to see Medusa without looking at her directly. Medusa was beheaded by Perseus. From Medusa's blood (or neck in some sources), Pegasus (see page 147) and Chrysaor[18] were born, although they are frequently stated to be the children of Medusa and Poseidon (some versions specify that they were only born when Medusa's blood reached the sea). Her blood did more than birth her children: Athena took blood from Medusa's left side, which had the power to kill, and blood from her right side, which was able to restore life to the dead. Medusa's head was used to turn the Titan Atlas to stone. A snake from Medusa's head was given to Sterope of Tegea to protect her town; although the snake could not turn those who looked on it to stone, it was able to fill those who saw it with dread and fear or to create a storm that had the same effect on attackers.

Despite Medusa's traditional association with evil and monstrosity, many scholars theorize that the head of the Gorgon was used as an icon of protection. The image of Medusa has appeared in numerous temples and on shields to deter evil spirits. The icon of the Gorgon head has changed over time, becoming less monstrous by losing its fangs, serpent tongue, and beard, to appear more beautiful, conforming with the fashions of the Hellenistic period.

MERMAIDS

LOCATION: Worldwide

CONTENT WARNING: Death, cannibalism, suicide, genital mutilation

Wherever there is water, there is always a narrative of water spirits, deities, or creatures living within the depths. Some may be benevolent creatures, protecting mankind, while others seek human blood. The use of "mermaid" as recognized in the West has been influenced by the Greek sirens, who were originally half-bird women, transformed into half-fish women when Christianity began to influence and rewrite ancient narratives. Sirens were depicted in later works as beautiful women with a fish's tail from the waist down who could sing and lure sailors to their death with their hypnotizing song. They would live on rocky coasts and cliffsides and use their voices to shipwreck sailors and feast on their corpses.

One of the earliest depictions of a mermaid-like creature comes from ancient Assyria (c. 2600 to 609 BCE) and the goddess Atargatis. She fell in love with a mortal man, and when she became pregnant, she threw herself into a lake in shame. An alternative version states that she killed her mortal lover by accident. Atargatis was so beautiful, the water refused to let her drown, so instead her body was transformed into a fish while her head remained human. In some versions, she has a fish's tail from the waist down, and in others, she remains fully human but has a fish tail in addition to her legs.

Mermaids and their variations have always been associated with peril for men and as dangerous women or malevolent men. Following is a selection of mermaid tales from around the world.

EL NADDAHA

LOCATION: Egypt

CONTENT WARNING: Death and suicide

Seen under the full moon, the beautiful El Naddaha stands on the shores of the river Nile in a flowing white dress, waiting for a man to pass by. When she sees her victim, she calls his name in a hypnotic voice and

guides him into the Nile with her, where he inevitably drowns (and, according to some, is eaten by her). If her victim is part of a group of men, she will still call out to him, but it is possible that the other men may be able to restrain him and prevent his death. However, El Naddaha curses the men who prevented her kill, and they live a miserable, harrowing existence until they are driven to suicide. Some stories tell how El Naddaha can fall in love with a man and will take him to her underwater cavern, living with him and having sexual relations for months until paranoia grips her. In fear of losing her lover, she drowns him and buries his bones in the depths of her cavern.

Some stories specify that El Naddaha is a white woman. Combined with the fact that the narrative became popular in the 1950s, this leads many to believe that she is just an urban legend rather than a classical myth.

JENGU/MIENGU

LOCATION: Cameroon

Miengu are water spirits and deities of Cameroon. *Miengu* is the plural form of *jengu*. In other areas of Cameroon, they are called *maengu* (plural) or a *liengu* (singular). Miengu are believed to share similarities with the West African Mami Wata figure, a water spirit, but are believed to predate her narratives. Meingu were created when a female spirit named Mojili (or Mojele) lost a bet with Moto, the ancestor of mankind, over who could build an everlasting fire. After her loss, Mojili was forced to leave the land and transformed her body in order to survive living in the sea. The miengu are descendants of Mojili.

Miengu are described as beautiful Black women with long hair in tight curls, a gap-toothed smile, and from the waist down, they have a long tail that changes to match the native fish species living in the water they reside in. Unlike European depictions of mercreatures, Miengu can have any body shape, from athletic to obese. Miengu can live in rivers as well as oceans. They bring good luck to any who worship them, they can cure diseases, and they act as a bridge between the human world and spirit world.

You can win the favor of a jengu by presenting them with jewelry and baubles, as they love to wear sparkling accessories and create a unique personal identity through fashion.

KATAW

LOCATION: Philippines
CONTENT WARNING: Death

Kataws are typically benevolent creatures and, unlike the European version of mermaids, retain their human legs and can walk on land. They have gills but can still breathe on land without any problems. They are kind and aid those who require help, blending into society as good Samaritans.

However, always show gratitude for their help; if you offend them, kataws can bewitch you to enter the nearest body of water and drown.

Kataws are at the top of the hierarchy of all water creatures and elementals in the ocean, as they can control the ocean tides, waves, and currents. They also have the ability to turn water into ice.

NINGYO

LOCATION: Japan

Ningyo live in large bodies of water and the seas surrounding Japan. They vary in appearance, ranging from a fish with the face of a monkey or human to a humanoid monster with large claws, fish features, and a fish's tail from the waist down. They are never depicted as beautiful or enchanting but rather as hideous beasts. That said, since the opening of Japan to European nations in the Edo period (1603 to 1867), there have been depictions of beautiful humans from the waist up with a fish's tail from the waist down; however, these are not generally considered to be ningyo. Ningyo cannot speak, but they have a soft, tuneful singing voice, like a skylark or flute. When a ningyo cries, they cry white pearls.

Catching a ningyo is considered bad luck and can bring earthquakes or tidal waves upon the villages of those who catch one. Despite this, people may attempt to catch them; it is said that if a woman takes a bite out of one, she will be granted eternal youth and beauty. Ningyos apparently taste delicious.

SAZAE-ONI

LOCATION: Japan
CONTENT WARNING: Sexual assault

Unlike other mermaids, sazae-oni have the bottom half of a turban snail, their "human" skin is textured like a snail's, and they are commonly depicted to have faces resembling the tip of a turban snail shell. Sazae-oni have two origin stories: Either they are turban snails who have reached the age of thirty and gained the ability to transform, or they are women who have been thrown into the ocean and transformed into turban snails; then, after thirty years as a snail, they become sazae-oni.

Sazae-oni appear to sailors as helpless maidens, tricking the sailors into letting them board their boat. Once aboard, the sazae-oni would kill everyone. There is a popular legend of the sazae-oni: A group of wealthy pirates rescue a young maiden, the crew have sex with her (versions vary on whether it was consensual or not), and she cuts or bites off the testicles of every man before returning to the ocean. From the ocean, she taunts the men and demands that they buy back their testicles from her. The pirates trade away all their gold in order to get their testicles. In Japan, testicles are sometimes called "golden balls," creating the punchline that they paid for gold with gold.

Sazae-oni may come on land and attack inns or houses near the shore. They appear to the owners as a woman but in the night reveal their true form and devour the inhabitants, leaving before the sun rises.

MINOTAUR ⊛

LOCATION: Crete, Greece
CATEGORY: Humanoid
CONTENT WARNING: Bestiality, sexual assault, death

In Ancient Greece, when King Minos competed with his brothers to rule the island of Crete, he boasted to his brothers that he was worthy of the throne because the gods would give him anything he requested. He prayed to Poseidon to give him a white bull, and in turn, he promised that he would sacrifice the bull in Poseidon's honor. A white bull rose from the ocean, and Minos's right to the throne was secured. However, Minos kept the holy bull for himself and sacrificed one of his ordinary bulls instead. Angered by his arrogance and deceit, Poseidon punished Minos by making his wife, Pasiphaë, fall in love with the white bull.

Several attempts to mate with the bull failed, so Pasiphaë commissioned Daedalus[19] to build a hollow cow for her to climb inside in order to fool the bull into mating with her. Nine months later, Pasiphaë gave birth to the Minotaur, half human and half bull, and named him Asterion. Pasiphaë nurtured the Minotaur, but as he grew, he became violent and savage and began eating humans. Minos demanded that Daedalus build a labyrinth to house the beast, and after it was completed, he kept Daedalus and his son, Icarus, prisoner to stop them from telling anyone about the Minotaur. The Minotaur was then trapped in the labyrinth.

When Minos began and won a war with Athens after the murder of his son, he demanded that seven young men and seven young women from Athens be sacrificed to the Minotaur every year (or every nine years, depending on the source). The wrath of the Minotaur ended when Theseus offered himself as a sacrifice with the intention of killing the Minotaur to end the suffering of the people of Athens (and to improve his hero status). When Thesus arrived in Crete, Minos's daughter Ariadne fell in love with him and begged Daedalus for a solution to the labyrinth's puzzle. Daedalus obliged, and Theseus entered the labyrinth with a ball of yarn that would allow him to navigate his way back out of the maze. Theseus overpowered and slew the Minotaur and married Ariadne after he left the labyrinth. (The marriage lasted only days before Theseus left her on an island; she then married the god Dionysus).

The Minotaur is described to be half bull and half man with no specification as to which half was bull and which half was man. He is typically depicted with the body of a man and the head and tail of a bull. Some artworks depict the Minotaur to resemble a centaur, with a bull's body, a human torso and arms where the bull's neck would be, and the head of a bull on top of a human neck.

PEGASUS ⭐

LOCATION: Greece
CATEGORY: Monster
CONTENT WARNING: Death, animal death

Son of Poseidon and Medusa (see page 134), Pegasus was born from the wound left after Medusa's decapitation at the hands of Perseus. Despite his brutal entry to the world, Pegasus has always been depicted as a naïve, gentle, and kind creature who strives to help others. Like his father, Pegasus could create spring water by striking the earth with his hoof, and he created a spring on Mount Helicon for the Muses.[20] He is always depicted as a white stallion with large, feathered wings.

With Athena's help, the monster slayer Bellerophon tamed Pegasus with a golden bridle. Together, Bellerophon and Pegasus were able to protect Lycia from the Amazons[21] and Solymi[22] and slay the Chimera.[23] Bellerophon was overcome with pride, believing he was above mortal men and that he deserved to be deified and sit with the gods. He mounted Pegasus and began to ascend to Mount Olympus, the home of the gods, but Zeus sent a gadfly to sting Pegasus, causing Bellerophon to be thrown from his back and fall to his death.

Pegasus finally reached Mount Olympus, where Zeus stabled him and tasked him with the role of pulling his chariot and carrying his thunderbolts. Pegasus served Zeus for years before passing away. Zeus honored Pegasus by transforming his body into a constellation so that he would always remain with them.

Cory says: I was raised with horses, so naturally at a young age I was drawn to the fantastical equines of myth and tall tale. Some of my earliest experiences with drawing were doodling horses on dot matrix printer paper. It was nostalgic to return to a creature that I had loved dearly as a child.

PSOGLAV

LOCATION: Bosnia and Montenegro
CATEGORY: Monster
CONTENT WARNING: Cannibalism

This iron-toothed beast stems from Balkan mythology. Psoglavs are nocturnal creatures and are intolerant of sunlight. During the day, they hide in abandoned mines or caves, where they hoard gemstones and riches. Once the sun has set, these beasts leave their caves and feast on human flesh. If unable to find live prey, psoglavs will dig up fresh corpses to sate their hunger.

The psoglav is described as a man with a dog's head, a single eye in the middle of their forehead, and iron teeth. Their hands are clawed, and they have the legs of a horse. They are said to smell of rotting flesh given how frequently they venture into graveyards.

In Russian and Serbian tales of the psoglav, the creature is called a psoglavi. Unlike the Balkan variant, they do not have iron teeth, a singular eye, or the legs of a horse. However, both versions are depicted as evil demonic creatures who feast upon humans. In the Russian and Serbian stories, psoglavi trick women into marrying them and then force them to cook human children for their dinner.

QILIN

LOCATION: China
CATEGORY: Monster

A qilin appearance signifies the birth or death of a great and kind ruler or a wise scholar. Qilin are commonly nicknamed the "Chinese unicorn" by Westerners for their peaceful nature and association with good luck. They are so gentle that they walk on clouds, for they do not wish to harm even a blade of grass beneath their hooves. However, because they are protectors of good and able to see into the hearts of man to decide upon their true nature, qilin will protect innocent people by incinerating those who seek to harm them with their fiery breath.

The story of the qilin spread across Asia; different regions and countries have their own variations on the appearance of the beast. During China's Jin dynasty (1115 to 1234 CE), they appeared as horses or bulls covered in scales with the head of a dragon, shrouded in fire and smoke. During the Ming dynasty (1368 to 1644 CE), the appearance evolved to include horns and ornamental flames. During the Qing dynasty (1644 to 1912 CE), they had the head of a dragon, antlers of a deer, legs of an ox, tail of a lion, and were covered in fishlike scales.

Some Chinese art depicts qilin as based on giraffes after an event in the Ming dynasty when the Yongle Emperor was presented with two giraffes and told they were qilin, as giraffes were an unknown creature at the time (the most famous piece of art depicting this scene is *Giraffe with Two Keepers*). Generally, Japanese depictions of qilin are similar to China's but favor a deerlike appearance over horses or bulls. Artwork depicts them as a dragon with a deer body, the tail of an ox, and occasionally with a backward curving horn. Vietnamese descriptions share features with the Chinese qilin; however, their depictions can include the head of a tiger or dragon, the mane of a lion, and can have either two antlers or a horn. In Korea, qilin are creatures with a beautiful mane, the body of a deer or horse, and the tail of an ox.

ROMPO

LOCATION: India and South Africa
CATEGORY: Monster

The tales of rompos speak of a creature with the head of a hare, human ears, the front legs of a badger, the hind legs of a bear, and a skeletal torso. These hybrid beasts have an unusual quirk: As they feast on human flesh, they sing and croon to themselves in delight. Rompos are shy and believed not to target living humans when possible. They are cautious when approaching corpses, surveying the area for danger before advancing. If a rompo is threatened or cornered, they are believed to have chameleonlike abilities, able to camouflage with their surroundings or to mimic the coloring of a predator.

It is believed the myth of the rompo originates from a misunderstanding of Old World porcupines.

RUSALKA

LOCATION: Eastern Europe
CATEGORY: Spirits
CONTENT WARNING: Death and suicide

Before the 1800s, rusalki were pagan spirits who were celebrated through the form of dance for their ability to bring water to fields, helping crops grow. After the 1830s, they began to be referred to as demonesses who were considered evil and malicious, similar to the vodyanoy (see page 164) and who would torment mankind.

Rusalka folklore blends with Christian and Greek mythology after the 1800s, as they were frequently referred to as "unclean," believed to be the souls of those who died and were not baptized. Some regions have stories of young village men falling in love with the spirits, who would show them their underwater palaces before allowing the men to take them home. The rusalka would allow herself to be baptized if the man offered to marry her, and after her baptism, she would be transformed into a human.

The more popular stories in contemporary society describe rusalki as the miserable spirits of women who were murdered or who committed suicide due to the actions of men. They were vengeful, taking the appearance of beautiful women to lure men toward the water, where they would proceed to drown them, drawing parallels to the Greek sirens and mermaids (see page 136). A rusalka would only be released from her spectral existence if she were able to drown the man who wronged her. Another belief is that a rusalka could only live out the remaining days she would have had on Earth as a mortal, had she not died prematurely and become a rusalka—similar to the bean nighe (see page 65).

Before the Soviet Union began to suppress the local beliefs in the 1930s, locals would celebrate the first week of June as Rusalki Week. During this week, entering any body of water was believed to be a guaranteed death sentence. At night, the rusalki would leave the water, play in the birch and willow trees, and dance in a circle under the moon (linking back to circular pagan dancing prior to the 1800s).

Anyone who witnessed the dance would end up joining in and dancing until they died. At the end of the week, locals would perform a ritual to banish the rusalki back into the water.

Depending on the region, rusalki adopt traits from localized beliefs. Some believe rusalki are malicious toward women instead of men, while some believe that they can be temporarily sated with gifts of scarves and jewelry, and others believe that they can be repelled by a crucifix. Even their origins cannot be agreed upon, with some suggesting that rusalki may be the spirits of women who died before losing their virginity. In parts of Ukraine, they believe that the rusalki who live near the Danube River are kind, friendly, and benevolent, while those who live where crops struggle to grow are malicious and cruel.

SIMURGH ⭐

LOCATION: Iran
CATEGORY: Monster
CONTENT WARNING: Death

Originating in Persian mythology, the Simurgh is a great and wise creature, supposedly so old that she has seen the destruction of Earth three times over. Some accounts state that she must plunge herself into flames every seventeen hundred years in order to be reborn, drawing parallels to the stories of the phoenix. She is a giant beast, able to fly while carrying the body of a whale. Early depictions give her the body of a peacock, the head of a hound, and lion claws, while later artworks depict her as increasingly birdlike. Some less popular images give her the head of a human and four wings.

The Simurgh is a divine creature, representing the connection between the sky and the earth. She lives in the Tree of Life, and when she first took flight, seeds showered down to Earth and sprouted into the first plants. She is revered as motherly and kind by nature, raising several heroes in her nest; however, she has resorted to eating humans in times of great hunger or if she deems the individuals to be evil.

The Simurgh is often compared to the phoenix of Greek mythology due to the rebirth tale. She is considered by many to be synonymous with the Anqa of Arabian mythology due to similar appearances and the seventeen-thousand-year lifespan. Some consider her to be the equivalent of the Simargl in Slavic mythology and the Konrul in Turkic mythology.

SIRIN

LOCATION: Russia
CATEGORY: Humanoid
CONTENT WARNING: Death

Inspired by the Greek sirens and harpies (see page 129), the sirin are traditionally depicted as owls with female human faces and breasts, and some versions show them to have peacock tails. They are usually wearing a crown or have some form of halolike light behind their heads.

Sirins would sing for the saints; however, their songs would drive mortals into a trance in which they would follow the singer across the world until they died (similar to the siren song of Greek mythology). Despite their fatal song, they are seen as a force of good and a blessing for the virtuous. In the 1600s, their song changed to one of hope and happiness but could only be heard by those who were already happy. The sirins are swift and fast fliers and were believed to be difficult to catch as a metaphor for the difficulty in chasing and capturing human happiness.

SPHINX

LOCATION: Turkey, Egypt, Greece
CATEGORY: Monster
CONTENT WARNING: Death and suicide

The most famous sphinx is the Great Sphinx of Giza, a limestone statue of the mythical beast that has established the image of the sphinx as Egyptian. However, older imagery of the sphinx can be found in Turkey, but we know very little about the sphinxes and their stories before the narratives of the ancient Greek. We can theorize, as there are parallels between the Egyptian and Greek stories, and the Greek took the image from Egypt in the first place. The Egyptian sphinx is typically seen as benevolent and gentle in contrast to the ruthless and ferocious Grecian sphinx. The Greek presented the sphinx as female, while Egyptian sphinxes were traditionally male. Egypt presented the sphinx as a species, whereas Greek mythology stated that she was a singular entity.

The Greek depiction of the Sphinx is the most popular: With the body of a lion and the face of a human, they gave her wings, and in some versions, the tail ends with a snake's head. The Sphinx of Greek mythology is best known for her riddles. She guards the city of Thebes and only grants entry to those who can solve her riddle. Those who failed were devoured by her. Her most famous riddle was, "Which creature has one voice and yet becomes four-footed and two-footed and three-footed?" with the answer, "man—who crawls on all fours as a baby, then walks on two feet as an adult, and then uses a walking stick in old age." When Oedipus solved her riddle, the Sphinx threw herself to her death. This is believed to be a metaphor for the death of old religions and the rise of the Olympian deities, as the Greeks acknowledged that she predated their beliefs.

The sphinxes of Asia still play a role in historical religious iconography. In southern India, the sphinx is placed near temple entrances to chase away evil spirits and sins. In Sri Lanka, the sphinx can be seen on banners, and it is the guardian of northern travel. In Thailand, the sphinx has a protective role; it is often depicted with the upper body of a human and the lower body of a lion, and they are found in pairs of male and female.

Rachel C. says: I've always loved how common human-animal hybrids are in mythology. The sphinx is most often associated with Egypt but also shows up in Greece, India, Thailand, and Sri Lanka, each with different traditions and iconography. The oldest recorded sphinx was found in Turkey and is over ten thousand years old. I love how regal the sphinx is portrayed and wanted to use rich, warm, bright colors to convey this.

UMIBŌZU

LOCATION: Japan
CATEGORY: Yokai
CONTENT WARNING: Death

The umibōzu, orumibōzu, is a sea-dwelling yokai that has only ever been seen from the shoulders up. The presence of an umibōzu can change a calm, quiet night, transforming it into a wild, turbulent oceanic storm as the creature rises up. They will attempt to destroy any ship or boat either with either a single blow or by dismantling the boat piece by piece. Alternative stories show the umibōzu demanding a barrel from the crew, which it then uses to flood the ship. One way to avoid this fate is to give the creature a barrel with no top or bottom, causing water to fall out of the barrel before it can sink the ship.

Umibōzu are believed to be the angry spirits of priests who were drowned at sea by villagers. Others state that they are the ancestors of all ocean yokai and are ancient sea monsters. Umibōzu are described to be inky black with no distinct features except for two large eyes and a bald head. Less common depictions show them as more serpentine or dragon-like.

UNICORN

LOCATION: Indus Valley (present-day Afghanistan, Pakistan, and India)

CATEGORY: Monster

Tales of unicorns date back to 4000 BCE to the Indus Valley during the Mesopotamian era. The presentation of the unicorn differs across the ages and the multiple civilizations in which they appear. They are typically presented as a cloven-hoofed animal with a singular horn growing from their forehead. Earlier depictions give unicorns the body of bulls, antelopes, deer, or goats; the image of the unicorn as a horse was created during the Middle Ages. Later added to Christian texts, unicorns could only be caught by virginal women. The beast would lie in her lap, transfixed by her purity and unaware of the surrounding hunters. This hunting method was used as a metaphor for the betrayal of Jesus.

Across several cultures, the unicorn horn (called an alicorn) was a highly valued commodity. In 400 BCE Greece, using an alicorn as a drinking vessel would render any poison in the drink harmless to the drinker. The idea of an alicorn as a purifying tool continued through the 1600s, when artwork of unicorns drinking from water sources showed the horn touching the water as they drank, supposedly an act of cleansing contaminated water. The alicorn has been cited as a historical cure for rubella, measles, the plague, rabies, "falling-sickness" (epilepsy), smallpox, headaches, "pains," and weak hearts; it can also be used as an antidote for poisons and as an aphrodisiac. Doctors in the 1100s believed the liver of a unicorn could be mixed with egg yolk to cure leprosy. A belt made of unicorn leather could protect wearers from the plague, while shoes made from unicorn leather could protect the wearer from various foot and leg ailments.

Unicorns in eastern Asia are portrayed as having multicolored bodies, and their very presence is deemed a great honor for anyone who sees them. The Russian unicorn has a forked prong on the end of its horn. In Chile, you can find El Camahueto, a creature similar to a unicorn, described as a bull with a single horn on its forehead. China has its own creature similar to a unicorn, the qilin (see page 151). The Democratic Republic of the Congo has the Abada (see page 111).

VODYANOY ⭐

LOCATION: Balkans
CATEGORY: Spirit—shapeshifter
CONTENT WARNING: Death

Floating on a log down the rivers of the Balkans, you may be unfortunate enough to cross paths with the Vodyanoy, an evil spirit who loves to drown humans. He floats along rivers, waiting for bathers to enter the water at sunset. If anyone enters the water without making the sign of the cross, he attacks, pulling them under the water and drowning them. Drownings were frequently blamed on the spirit. When angered, he would cause dams to collapse, flood rivers and farmland, and destroy watermills.

Vodyanoy is supposedly a shapeshifter but traditionally took the form of an old, naked man with green skin and hair. His skin is slick with algae and moss, mottled with black scales and dirt. He has fiery red eyes, webbed hands, and a fish's tail. His face has frog-like features, with some depictions showing him as a frog who can walk on two legs.

In Russian folklore, the Vodyanoy is not a singular being but a species that answers to a ruler named Tsar Vodyanik, who can fly on a black storm cloud and create new rivers and lakes with his large club. In the western regions of the Balkans, they are called the vodníci, who look more like humans but have gills and wear bizarre, patchy, and dirty clothes. They may linger out of water for long periods of time, provided they keep damp, and they may be spotted by their wet appearance. The vodníci can be both good and evil; some may help local fishermen in exchange for tobacco. In their free time (when they're not drowning people), they enjoy smoking and playing cards. All vodníci own a prized teapot that they use to store the souls of those they drown. Opening the lids of these teapots will release those trapped inside.

WANIGUCHI

LOCATION: Japan
CATEGORY: Yokai

The waniguchi is a rascally little yokai that has been documented in writing as far back as the Edo period (1603 to 1867), appearing in the *HyakkiYagyō* (*"Night Parade of One Hundred Demons"*). The waniguchi is named after a waniguchi gong that hangs in Shinto shrines. A waniguchi gong is a large, hollow, disc-shaped gong with a slit through the middle that looks like a mouth when viewed from the side. In Japanese, the word *waniguchi* has two translations: The first is "shrine bell" and the second is "crocodile mouth." The waniguchi creature was inspired by the dual definitions of the word, creating a shrine bell, crocodile-mouth creature!

When a waniguchi gong transforms into a yokai, the gong becomes the creature's head, and it sprouts a reptilian body and tail from the back. According to the mythos, the waniguchi can open its gong-mouth like a crocodile.

ZHENG

LOCATION: China
CATEGORY: Monster

The Zheng is a ferocious and malevolent beast and is the male counterpart to the female Ning. He is illustrated to have the body of a leopard, a singular horn on his head, and his tail has been split into five individual tails. Zheng lives high up in the mountains, where the high altitude makes it difficult for others to breathe. Thus it is theorized that he does not require oxygen or may have a biological system that allows him to go for long periods of time without oxygen. Because he lives in high, cold mountains, his red fur is incredibly thick and sought after, as it may carry magical properties.

When hunting, the Zheng uses his five tails in a display to distract his prey. He can snap his tails together to create the sound of stones striking against each other.

The Zheng is not the only multi-tailed feline in Chinese mythology. There is also the Huan, which resembles a lynx or bobcat. The Huan has three long tails and a single eye in the center of its forehead. The Huan scares away misfortune, and wearing its fur as a coat could cure jaundice.

APPENDIXES

NOTES

1. **CRYPTID**—Oxford English Dictionary, s.v. "cryptid, n.", July 2023. https://doi.org/10.1093/OED/2268506511

2. **CRYPTID**—The Mothman of Point Pleasant. (2017). [film] Directed by S. Breedlove. Produced by Small Town Monsters.

3. **GLOBSTER**—Michael Newton's book *Hidden Animals: A Field Guide to Batsquatch, Chupacabra, and Other Elusive Creatures* has an excellent breakdown of globsters that have appeared over the centuries.

4. **LOCH NESS MONSTER**—To list a few variants: Bear Lake Monster (Idaho/Utah, United States), Bessie (Lake Erie, United States and Canada), Bohzo (Wisconsin, United States), Caddy (British Columbia, Canada), Champy (New York/Vermont, United States, and Quebec, Canada), Chessie (Chesapeake Bay, United States), Illie (Alaska, United States), Lake Tianchi Monster (China and North Korea), Lake Van Monster (Van, Turkey), Lariosauro (Lombardy, Italy), Manipogo (Manitoba, Canada), Memphré (Vermont, United States, and Quebec, Canada), Mokele-mbembe (Congo Basin, African continent), Nahuelito (Patagonia, Argentina), Ogopogo (British Columbia, Canada), Pepie (Minnesota/Wisconsin, United States), Selma (Telemark, Norway), and Tessie (California/Nevada, United States).

5. **BUSCHGROßMUTTER**—Frau Holle is believed to be a protectress of agriculture and women's crafts or a demonic figure in some texts; in others, she is either the leader of the huldra (forest nymphs), which were seductive forest women, or the only huldra that existed. The huldra are said to be protectors of the forest.

6. **BUSCHGROßMUTTER**—Perchta is a pagan goddess who has more in common with Krampus (a creature who punishes children who have been naughty while the good children get gifts from Saint Nicholas/Santa Claus) than Frau or Buschgroßmutter. Perchta is concerned with the spinning of yarn and domestic tidiness. Should you have failed to spin all your yarn by January 6, she may set fire to unspun fibers, but if your house is a mess as well *and* you've failed to leave her a bowl of porridge, she will disembowel you and replace your organs with rocks and straw. During her hunts, she flies with her army along with the souls of unbaptized children.

7. **CAT SÍDHE**—The King of Cats: A farmer traveling home pauses when he sees a procession of eight black cats with white chest spots carrying a coffin with a royal crest. The cats proclaim, "The king is dead," and one

tells the farmer, "Tell Tom Tildrum that Tim Toldrum is dead." Confused and intrigued, the farmer returns home to his wife and cat and tells his wife what he witnessed. Upon hearing the story, his cat sits up and says, "What?! Old Tim dead! Then I'm the King o' the Cats!" and climbs up the chimney, never to be seen again.

8. **CÙ SÌTH**—Cŵn Annwn: The spectral hounds of Annwn (a paradise Otherworld), who were later believed to belong to the fairy king. It was believed that hearing the howl of the Cŵn Annwn was a sign of your approaching death. Like many creatures in mythology and folklore, to hear loud snarls and growls signified that the beasts were far away, whereas when they were soft and quiet, the Cŵn Annwn were nearby. Cŵn Annwn were also associated with migrating geese, as the nighttime honks were misconstrued as dog barks.

   Cŵn Annwn are associated with the Wild Hunt that happens on significant nights of the year, when they hunt and run down treacherous criminals before tearing them apart. Cŵn Annwn would escort souls of the dead to the Otherworld. Christians later demonized the hounds, calling them "Hounds of Hell," although Annwn is a medieval place of delight and eternal youth and is free of disease.

9. **HERNE THE HUNTER**—The Wild Hunt has been associated with a number of European folktales. The Hunt is usually led by a figure with similarities to Odin, and his fellow hunters are fairies, elves, or specters of the dead. The hunters would ride on black horses or black rams and have giant black hounds (sometimes described as hellhounds or creatures like Cŵn Annwn). It was believed that any mortal who witnessed a Wild Hunt would either die or be abducted into the fairy world, never to be seen again.

10. **AO AO**—Tau: A spirit of evil from Guaraní mythology, Tau is sometimes referred to as "The Evil Spirit." He became smitten by Kerena, a beautiful human and daughter of a chieftain. Tau kidnapped Kerena, and it is unclear due to the oral traditions whether they were married or whether Kerena was raped by Tau and bore seven children, five of which were monsters.

11. **BAKE-KUJIRA**—Passive whaling would occur in Japan when whales would swim too close to the shore and become stranded. Whales were so beneficial for communities, they were seen as extensions of the gods, and their remains would be ceremoniously buried. Further reading into the role of whales in Japanese folklore and history is encouraged!

12. **CUÉLEBRE**—Xana: A type of fairy that would trick and ruin the evil plots of Ojáncanu (a cyclops). Xanas are depicted as fair maidens with long blonde hair who sing at night. Those of fair heart who hear her singing

will be overcome with a sense of love and joy, while those without will feel as if they are being choked and may go insane. There are parallels between xanas and the depiction of lamias (creatures that are half woman and, from the waist down, half snake); however, this is probably due to the blending of Asturian and Roman mythology. There is a second type of xanas that is described as evil and will steal children (linking to the original story of Lamia, who later birthed the lamia species).

13. **HARPY**—Erinyes, better known as the Furies, are supernatural beings of vengeance who lived beneath the earth. They were created from the drops of blood that hit the earth when Cronus castrated his father, Uranus.

14. **LESHY**—Veles is the Slavic god of cattle, wildlife, the harvest, trickery, wealth, music, magic, the earth, water, and the underworld. The Leshy comes from the same mythology, and people believed either that Leshy was an earthly representation of Veles or that he was a servant.

15. **LESHY**—The Erl-King, or Erlkönig, first appeared in a poem by Johann Gottfried von Herder called "Erlkönigs Tochter" (1778), which was an adaptation of "Hr. Oluf Han Rider" (1739)—both of these poems focus on his daughter. The Erl-King himself appeared in Johann Wolfgang von Goethe's poem "Erlkönig" (1782), which tells the tale of a spirit that preys upon children for fun and snatches them away to the land of the dead. In Angela Carter's *The Bloody Chamber* (1979), the Erl-King is a malevolent spirit who seduces young women before turning them into birds that he keeps in cages when he becomes bored of them.

16. **MEDUSA**—Critics speculate as to why Athena punished Medusa and not Poseidon. One theory is that, due to the hierarchy of the pantheon and the fact that Poseidon was her uncle, Athena was unable to punish him but instead gave Medusa the ability to protect herself. This theory falls apart because Athena later gives Perseus the weapons to kill Medusa.

A different theory from classical studies scholar Jane Harrison states that Medusa was originally a goddess in a theology that was then overturned by the Greek mythos (and that she and her two sisters formed a triumvirate). Some theorize that Athena was created from the narratives of Medusa, as the two have similar imagery and share a multitude of qualities.

The gorgon face was actually a mask used in religious ceremonies, and the priestesses would "hiss" to ward off people who would try to interfere with the ritual. Scholar Patricia Monaghan adds that the snakes in Medusa's hair could have originally been rays of light. The conclusion is that Medusa's tale is used to reinforce patriarchal ideology of victim blaming, depicting women as inferior to the whims of men, and to pit women against one another.

17. **MEDUSA**—Perseus: Perseus was sent by his adoptive uncle, King Polydectes (who wanted Perseus dead so that he could seduce his mother without Perseus preventing him), to slay and bring back the head of Medusa, a task his uncle believed would be impossible. Perseus entered Medusa's cave and beheaded her. When he returned, he discovered that his mother had been threatened (and, in some sources, raped) by Polydectes. Perseus confronted Polydectes while he was holding court. Surprised at Perseus's return, he was unprepared for Perseus to produce Medusa's head, which turned Polydectes and every courtier to stone. Perseus handed the kingdom to the man who had cared for him and his mother since they had arrived on the island years before.

18. **MEDUSA**—Chrysaor was a regular human who supposedly became the king of Iberia.

19. **MINOTAUR**—Daedalus is famous within Greek Mythology for his excellent inventions and engineering skills. He invented the labyrinth to contain the Minotaur and was imprisoned in a tower to ensure he would remain silent about the origin of the Minotaur. He is the father of Icarus, and when escaping prison, he crafted the wings that Icarus used to fly too close to the sun (against his father's warnings).

20. **PEGASUS**—The Muses are nine goddesses of inspiration. Each Muse has their own domain, and they are frequently praised in literature for their artistic roles and for allowing knowledge to be passed on through oral tradition. You have Calliope of epic poetry, Clio of history, Erato of love poetry, Euterpe of music, song, and lyrical poetry, Melpomene of tragedies, Polyhymnia of comedy, Terpsichore of dance, Thalia of comedy, and Urania of astrology.

21. **PEGASUS**—The Amazons were a race or tribe of talented warrior women.

22. **PEGASUS**—The Solymi were a tribe who had ancestry linking back to Zeus's son, Solymus.

23. **PEGASUS**—The Chimera is a fire-breathing monster with three heads; one head is a goat, the second head is a lion, and both of those come out of the neck, which is attached to a body of a lion. The third head—that of a snake—appears at the tip of the tail. Some versions of the Chimera depict it to have wings. The Chimera is a sibling to Cerberus, the three-headed dog who guards the gates to the underworld. "Chimera" is often used as an adjective to describe creatures that are made up of multiple animal parts.

CONTRIBUTOR BIOGRAPHIES

ELDRITCH RACH (author and main illustrator)

Name: Rachel Quinney

Description: Reclusive and hard to find, Rachel is a shy artist and literature teacher. Generally nocturnal, they enjoy a good (or terrible) pun and can often be found singing silly songs to entertain themself. Rachel's passion for the strange and unusual has stayed with them since childhood, and now they spend their time drawing cryptids like Mothman and Nessie. You can lure Rachel out of their hiding place by leaving an offering of chocolate or washi tape.

Favorite cryptid: Tizzie-whizie

Primary website: www.eldritchrach.com

Social media handle: @eldritchrach

Online store: etsy.com/uk/shop/EldritchRach

BAVARII

Description: Native to the lush lands of Lower Bavaria, Bavarii can be often spotted around historic sights, museums, and pieces of art, often traveling far distances for them. He is also known to do art himself: Pictures about fantasy, *Dungeons & Dragons,* and hot guys are the most common subjects. An easy way to lure out this goat-headed creature is with his favorite diet: coffee and cake.

Favorite cryptid: Kraken

Social media handle: @KnightKnack

Appears on page 24 with the Goatman and page 145 with the Minotaur

CAITI GRAY

Name: Caitlyn Gray

Description: Caitlyn is an illustrator and cartoonist interested in science and storytelling. As a child, she was constantly told to stop daydreaming by her teachers, so she set out to become a cartoonist out of stubbornness. She works on everything, from webcomics and book jackets to character design and educational art. Despite her love of zoology, she has been known to go through zoos shaming the animals for being ugly.

Favorite cryptid: Shug Monkey

Website: https://bttdb.thecomicseries.com/

Social media handle: @anintrinsicgray

Appears on the bottom of page 93 with the Shug Monkey

CORY MCGOWAN

Name: Cory McGowan

Description: Character designer, illustrator, world builder, and round-the-clock monster fan. Be wary of when they start cracking jokes—once they start, they won't leave you alone until you laugh.

Favorite cryptid: Kitsune—a yokai from Japanese folklore

Primary website: crowcouncil.weebly.com

Social media handle: @CoryCatte

Online store: etsy.com/shop/crowcouncil

Appears on page 102 with the Wulver and page 146 with the Pegasus

FUNGII DRAWS

Name: Fungii Draws
Description: Item #: SCP-■■
Object class: Euclid
Description: SCP-■■ has the appearance of a 30- to 40-year-old human and enjoys creating colorful artwork on a tablet that they are always seen carrying around. It often complains of a sore back; however, X-rays have revealed that there is nothing anomalous about their spine, besides what one would typically expect from a human who spends most of their time in a bad drawing posture. SCP-■■ has asked that it be mostly referred to as "Fungii Draws" when talking about its artwork.

Favorite cryptid: Tsuchinoko
Social media handle: @fungiidraws
Online store: fungiidraws.storenvy.com
Appears on page 168 with the Zheng

HALLALAWEEN (artist and editor of the Kickstarter edition)

Name: La
Description: The La is a strange fey creature of words and colors. Rarely seen in the light of day or the dark of night, unless your eyes are closed. They are known to haunt the dreams of friends with the stories they weave or, far more rarely, delight dreams with colorful knickknacks and images. That is, unless there is food, and in that case, dream or nightmare, they're there to be your best friend and eat anything shared (or not so shared).

Favorite cryptid: Hopkinsville Goblin
Social media handle: @hallalaween
Online store: etsy.com/shop/hallalaween
Appears on page 2 with the Bigfoot, page 72 with the Cat Sídhe, page 78 with the Grimalkin, page 91 with the Selkie, page 110 with the Abada, page 142 with the Sazae-oni, page 150 with the Qilin, and page 163 with the Unicorn

HARI CONNER

Name: Hari Conner

Description: Hari is an award-winning author and illustrator of LGBT+ and fantasy comics and game-books. Sightings usually occur in dark mountain forests in the Scottish Highlands around the full moon.

Favorite cryptid: Tsuchinoko

Website: hari-illustration.com

Social media handle: @haridraws

Appears on page 104 with the Ya-te-veo and Carnivorous Flora

JUNIJWI

Name: JuniJwi

Description: They are a nocturnal creature lured easily by coffee, honey, and the color orange. Salmon can be left out at night for them, and they will return the gift with drawings and video game coding.

Favorite cryptid: Rat King—a rare phenomenon when rats become joined together by their tails and continue to exist as a large, singular entity.

Primary website: crowcouncil.weebly.com

Social media handle: @junijwi

Online store: etsy.com/shop/crowcouncil

Appears on page 156 with the Simurgh

LYNDSEY GREEN ILLUSTRATION

Name: Lyndsey Green

Description: Lyndsey Green is a freelance illustrator whose work is inspired by her passion for wildlife and her love of fantasy and folklore. She particularly enjoys drawing the weird and wonderful animals, such as binturongs and fruit bats, while helping to raise awareness of endangered species and environmental conservation. She also loves to put her own spin on strange creatures from myth by combining different species of animals that live in similar terrains.

Favorite cryptid: Hard to choose, but probably the wolpertinger!

Primary website: lyndseygreen.co.uk

Social media handles: @lyndseythefox and @lyndseyillustration

Online store: etsy.com/shop/lyndseygreen

Appears on page 56 with the Wolpertinger

MORRIGHAN CORBEL

Name: Morrighan Corbel

Description: A hearth and home spirit, this Morrighan, unlike her bloodthirsty Irish counterpart (the goddess of war and death), enjoys her peace and quiet. Wielding her weapons of graphite and strangely textured rocks, she weaves eerie and atmospheric illustrations, bringing to life spirits and stories both great and terrible. She has recently completed a yearlong folklore project and enjoys illustrating books and covers. When she isn't drawing, Morrighan enjoys collecting old relics, usually photographs, and sometimes ventures out of her host home to find new and interesting places to eat.

Favorite cryptid: The Beast of Bodmin Moor—a large black cat that was sighted between 1983 and 1996 in the United Kingdom

Website: morrighancorbel.co.uk

Social media handle: @morrighancorbel

Appears on page 82 with Herne the Hunter

RACHEL CUSH

Name: Rachel Cush

Description: This small gremlin-like creature rarely leaves its cave; it's often covered in paint and has a voracious appetite for noodles and tea. It's found primarily in the Scottish Highlands and loves mythology, nature, and magic, often spending hours planning fantasy worlds, creatures, and stories. It can also be spotted at different comic events in the United Kingdom, attempting to communicate with human beings.

Favorite cryptid: This is a tough one! I love how many strange yokai there are, but I have a soft spot for selkies!

Primary website: craftymarten.com

Social media handle: @craftymarten

Online store: etsy.com/shop/craftymarten

Appears on page 85 with the Kelpie and page 160 with the Sphinx

TENGURINE

Name: Tengurine
Description: Often found in their nest and surrounded by reptiles, Teng only emerges on blood moons, occasionally with a new drawing or two.
Favorite cryptid: Chupacabra
Social media handle: @tengurine
Appears on page 9 with the Texas Chupacabra

ESTHER DE DAUW

Esther edited the Introduction for the Kickstarter.

REFERENCES

Alexander, S. (2014). *Fairies: The Myths, Legends, & Lore*. Adams Media Corporation.

Arcgis.com.(n.d.). "Bigfoot Culture and Belief of Sasquatch in the United States." [online] Available at: https://www.arcgis.com/apps/MapJournal/index.html?appid=a64e370436be48239ee334333522e851 [Accessed: August 30, 2023].

Astonishing Legends. (2016). "Ep 50-54: Mothman." [podcast] Available at: https://astonishinglegends.com/al-podcasts/2017/2/7/ep-050-mothman-part-1?rq=Mothman; https://astonishinglegends.com/al-podcasts/2017/2/7/ep-051-mothman-part-2?rq=Mothman; https://astonishinglegends.com/al-podcasts/2017/2/7/ep-052-mothman-part-3?rq=Mothman; https://astonishinglegends.com/al-podcasts/2017/2/7/ep-053-mothman-part-4?rq=Mothman; https://astonishinglegends.com/al-podcasts/2017/2/7/ep-054-mothman-part-5?rq=Mothman.

Atlas Obscura. (n.d.). "Goatman's Bridge." [online] Available at: https://www.atlasobscura.com/places/goatmans-bridge [Accessed: 2019].

Atlas Obscura. (n.d.). "Pope Lick Trestle Bridge." [online] Available at: https://www.atlasobscura.com/places/pope-lick-trestle-bridge [Accessed: 2019].

Atsma, A. (2017). "HARPIES (Harpyiai)—Bird-Women Monsters & Storm Spirits of Greek Mythology." [online] *Theoi.com*. Available at: https://www.theoi.com/Pontios/Harpyiai.html [Accessed: September 17, 2023].

Atsma, A. (2017). "SPHINX—Woman-Headed Lion of Greek Mythology." [online] *Theoi.com*. Available at: https://www.theoi.com/Ther/Sphinx.html [Accessed: September 17, 2023].

Bane, T. (2016). *Encyclopedia of Beasts and Monsters in Myth, Legend and Folklore*. McFarland & Company Publishers.

Bane, T. (2016). *Encyclopedia of Giants and Humanoids in Myth, Legend and Folklore*. McFarland & Company Publishers.

Bane, T. (2016). *Encyclopedia of Spirits and Ghosts in World Mythology*. McFarland & Company Publishers.

Benedict, A. (2018). "Cryptid Profile: Ningen." [blog] *The Pine Barrens Institute*. August 18, 2018. Available at: https://pinebarrensinstitute.com/cryptids/2018/8/18/cryptid-profile-ningen [Accessed: 2019].

Bergloff, A. (2018). "Werewolves that Fish and Fight in Battles: The Scottish Wulver and Irish Faoladh in Folklore." [blog] *#FolkloreThursday*. May 24, 2018. Available at: https://folklorethursday.com/legends/werewolves-that-fish-and-fight-in-battles-the-scottish-wulver-and-irish-faoladh-in-folklore/ [Accessed: 2019].

Blitz, M. (2015). "The Goatman—Or His Story, at Least—Still Haunts Prince George's County." [online] *Washingtonian*. Available at: https://www.washingtonian.com/2015/10/30/the-goatman-or-his-story-at-least-still-haunts-prince-georges-county/ [Accessed: 2019].

Boumis, R. (n.d.). "Snakes of the Gobi." [online] *Pets on Mom.com*. Available at: https://animals.mom.com/snakes-gobi-4056.html [Accessed: 2019].

Boyton, P. (2011). *Snallygaster: The Lost Legend of Frederick County*. Self-published, Lulu. (Originally published in 2008).

Braxton County Convention and Visitor's Bureau. (n.d.). "The Flatwoods Monster." [online] Available at: https://braxtonwv.org/the-flatwoods-monster/ [Accessed: 2019].

Cheatle, Julian. (2017). "Owlman." [online] *Paranormal Papers*. Available at: https://www.paranormalpapers.com/cryptozoology/owlman/ [Last modified March 6, 2023] [Accessed: 2019].

Cheung, T. (2009). *The Element Encyclopedia of Vampires: An A–Z of the Undead*. New York: Harper Element.

Chronicling America: Historic American Newspapers. (1891). "The Wichita Daily Eagle. [volume], September 04, 1891, Page 2, Image 2." [digitized newspaper] Library of Congress. Available at: https://chroniclingamerica.loc.gov/lccn/sn82014635/1891-09-04/ed-1/seq-2/.

Clark, C. (2012). "The Wonders of Unicorn Horns: Preventions and Cures for Poisoning." [blog] *The Recipes Project*. June 12, 2012. Available at: https://recipes.hypotheses.org/511.

Clark, J. (2013). *Unexplained!: Strange Sightings, Incredible Occurrences, and Puzzling Physical Phenomena*. 3rd ed. Detroit: Visible Ink Press.

Clark, J. (2015). "45 News Reports about the ASWANG since 2001." [online] *THE ASWANG PROJECT*. Available at: https://www.aswangproject.com/45-news-reports-aswang/ [Accessed: March 2019].

Cooke, Y. (2020). "The Story of the Lake District's Mythical Tizzie-Whizie." [online] *LancsLive*. Available at: https://www.lancs.live/news/local-news/story-lake-districts-mythical-tizzie-18732104 [Accessed: March 2023].

Daimler, M. (2014). *Pagan Portals—Fairy Witchcraft: A Neopagan's Guide to the Celtic Fairy Faith*. Alresford: Moon Books.

Davisson, Z. (2013). "Bakekujira and Japan's Whale Cults." [blog] 百物語怪談会 *HyakumonogatariKaidankai: Translated Japanese Ghost Stories and Tales of the Weird and Strange.* May 10, 2013. Available at: https://hyakumonogatari. com/2013/05/10/bakekujira-and-japans-whale-cults/ [Accessed: 2019].

Deekshithar, R. (2009). "Sphinxes in Indian Art and Tradition." [online] *Asianart.com.* Available at: https://www.asianart.com/articles/sphinxes/ index.html [Accessed: 2019].

DeLong, W. (2018). "The 'Dover Demon' Petrified Four Teens in a Small Town in 1977–and Remains Unexplained Today." [online] *All That's Interesting.* Available at: https://allthatsinteresting.com/dover-demon [Accessed: 2019].

Dhwty. (2018). "There Is More to the Sphinx Than You Find at Giza." [online] *Ancient Origins.* Available at: https://www.ancient-origins.net/artifacts-other-artifacts/sphinx-creature-0010658 [Accessed: 2019].

Dickinson, B. (2008). "Science (What Else?) Reveals the Secret of the Montauk Monster." [online] *Discover Magazine.* Available at: https://www. discovermagazine.com/the-sciences/science-what-else-reveals-the-secret-of-the-montauk-monster [Accessed: September 17, 2023].

Dictionary.com, s.v. "Grimalkin." [online] Available at: https://www.dictionary. com/browse/grimalkin [Accessed: September 17, 2023].

Eberhart, G. M. (2013). *Mysterious Creatures: A Guide to Cryptozoology— Volume 1.* 2nd revised ed. CFZ Press.

Eberhart, G. M. (2015). *Mysterious Creatures: A Guide to Cryptozoology— Volume 2.* CFZ Press.

Encyclopaedia Britannica, s.v. "Bunyip." [online] Available at: https://www. britannica.com/topic/bunyip [Last modified October 19, 2021] [Accessed: 2019].

Encyclopaedia Britannica, s.v. "Herne the Hunter." [online] Available at: https:// www.britannica.com/topic/Herne-the-Hunter [Last modified May 14, 2007] [Accessed: 2019].

Encyclopaedia Britannica, s.v. "Leshy." [online] Available at: https://www. britannica.com/topic/leshy[Last modified May 17, 2023] [Accessed: 2019].

Encyclopaedia Britannica, s.v. "Mi'rāj." [online] Available at: https://www. britannica.com/event/Miraj-Islam [Last modified August 29, 2023] [Accessed: 2019].

Encyclopaedia Britannica, s.v. "Qilin." [online] Available at: https://www. britannica.com/topic/qilin[Last modified February 2, 2023] [Accessed: 2019].

Encyclopaedia Britannica, s.v. "Vodyanoy." [online] Available at: https://www.britannica.com/topic/vodyanoy [Last modified September 2, 2022] [Accessed: 2019].

English National Opera (2020). "A Guide to the Slavic Folklore of Rusalka" [online]. Available at: https://www.eno.org/discover-opera/explore-more/a-guide-to-the-slavic-folklore-of-rusalka/.

Everything Dragon Shop. (2018). "Dragon Mythology: The Cuélebre." [online] Available at: https://www.everythingdragonshop.com/dragon-articles/dragon-mythology-the-cuelebre/ [Accessed: April 2019].

Fee, C. and Webb, J., eds. (2016). *American Myths, Legends, and Tall Tales.* Santa Barbara: ABC-CLIO.

Fisher, M. (2018). "Simurgh, the Mysterious Giant Healing Bird in Iranian Mythology." [online] *Ancient Origins.* Available at: https://www.ancient-origins.net/history/simurgh-mysterious-giant-healing-bird-iranian-mythology-0010030 [Accessed: 2019].

Frederick, M. (2012). "Leshy (Slavic Mythology)." [blog] *Myth and Lore.* April 16, 2012. Available at: http://mythandlore.blogspot.com/2012/04/leshy.html [Accessed: 2019].

Gaither, M. (2019). "The Egyptian Siren." [online] *The Advocate.* Forest Grove High School. Available at: https://fghsnews.com/1763/series/the-egyptian-siren/ [Accessed: 2019].

Garcia, B. (2013). "Medusa." [online] World History Encyclopedia. Available at: https://www.worldhistory.org/Medusa/ [Accessed: April 12, 2021].

Garcia, B. (2013). "Minotaur." [online] *World History Encyclopedia.* Available at: https://www.worldhistory.org/Minotaur/ [Accessed: September 17, 2023].

Gatehouse, J. (2014). *Monster Hunters Unlimited: Man-Monsters and Animal Horrors #3.* New York: Price Stern Sloan.

Geggel, L. (2018). "What the Heck Is This Hairy 'Sea Monster'?" [online] *Live Science.* Available at: https://www.livescience.com/62575-mysterious-sea-monster-philippines.html [Accessed: 2019].

Geller, Prof. (2016). "Bunyip." [forum] *Mythology.net.* November 18, 2016. Available at: https://mythology.net/mythical-creatures/bunyip/ [Accessed: 2019].

Geller, Prof. (2018). "Jackalope." [forum] *Mythology.net.* September 30, 2018. Available at: https://mythology.net/mythical-creatures/jackalope/ [Accessed: 2019].

Geller, Prof. (2018). "Leviathan." [forum] *Mythology.net.* September 29, 2018. Available at: https://mythology.net/monsters/leviathan/ [Accessed: 2019].

Geller, Prof. (2018). "Unicorn." [forum] *Mythology.net.* September 29, 2018. Available at: https://mythology.net/mythical-creatures/unicorn/ [Accessed: September 17, 2023].

Georgiou, M. (2018). "Tracking 129 years of the Flathead Lake Monster Sightings." [online] *NBC Montana.* Available at: https://nbcmontana.com/news/local/tracking-129-years-of-flathead-lake-monster-sightings [Accessed: March 2023].

Glennon, M. (2017). "Medusa in Ancient Greek Art." [online] The Metropolitan Museum of Art. Available at: https://www.metmuseum.org/toah/hd/medu/hd_medu.htm [Accessed: 2019].

Goldstein, J. (2014). *101 Amazing Mythical Beasts and Legendary Creatures.* Andrews UK Limited.

Greek Gods & Goddesses. (2017). "Harpies." [online] Available at: https://greekgodsandgoddesses.net/myths/harpies/ [Accessed: 2019].

Greekmythology.com. (2015). "Chimaera." [online] Available at: https://www.greekmythology.com/Myths/Creatures/Chimaera/chimaera.html [Accessed: 2019].

Greekmythology.com. (2021). "Medusa." [online] Available at: https://www.greekmythology.com/Myths/Creatures/Medusa/medusa.html [Accessed: 2019].

Greekmythology.com. (2021). "Minotaur." [online] Available at: https://www.greekmythology.com/Myths/Monsters/Minotaur/minotaur.html [Accessed: 2019].

Greekmythology.com. (2021). "Pegasus." [online] Available at: https://www.greekmythology.com/Myths/Creatures/Pegasus/pegasus.html [Accessed: 2019].

Greekmythology.com. (2021). "Sphinx." [online] Available at: https://www.greekmythology.com/Myths/Monsters/Sphinx/sphinx.html [Accessed: 2019].

Griffin, B. (n.d.). "The Legend of the Flatwoods Monster." [online] *West Virginia Department of Arts, Culture and History.* Available at: https://archive.wvculture.org/goldenseal/fall02/legend.html.

Hall, J. (2005). "The Cryptid Zoo: Shug Monkey." [online] *The Cryptid Zoo: A Menagerie of Cryptozoology.* Available at: http://www.newanimal.org/shugmonkey.htm [Accessed: September 17, 2023].

Hall, J. (2006). "The Cryptid Zoo: Dobhar-chu." [online] *The Cryptid Zoo. A Menagerie of Cryptozoology.* Available at: http://www.newanimal.org/dobhar.htm [Accessed: 2019].

Hanlon, T. (2013) "'Tailypo' and 'The Big Toe.'" [online] *AppLit's Annotated Index of Folktales.* Ferrum College, the National Endowment for the Humanities, and the Appalachian College Association. Available at: http://www2.ferrum.edu/applit//bibs/tales/tailypo.htm [Accessed: September 17, 2023].

Hare of the Rabbit (2017). *Jackalope Rabbit Breed – Wolpertinger – Skvader – Al-Miraj – Mayan Folktale – Knowledge – Lobelia.* [online] Castbox. Available at: https://castbox.fm/episode/Jackalope-Rabbit-Breed---Wolpertinger---Skvader---Al-Miraj---Mayan-Folktale---Knowledge---Lobelia-id466074-id50141850?country=us.

Harewood, F. (2015). "Timeline." [blog] *Roswell Rods–We Review the Facts & Myths.* December 16, 2015. Available at: http://roswellrods.com/ [Accessed: 2019].

Harrison, J. (1955). *Prolegomena to the Study of Greek Religion.* New York: Meridian Books.

Haslam, G. (n.d.). "1954, August 11: The Canvey Island Monsters." [online] *Anomalies: The Strange & Unexplained.* Available at: http://anomalyinfo.com/Stories/1954-august-11-canvey-island-monsters [Accessed: 2019].

Haslam, G. (n.d.). "Kraken: Myths, Legends, and History." [online] *Anomalies: The Strange & Unexplained.* Available at: http://anomalyinfo.com/Stories/kraken-myths legends-and-history [Accessed: 2019].

Heatherson, L. (2012). "The Canvey Island Monster: My Findings." [online] *Canvey Community Archive.* Available at: https://www.canveyisland.org/abc-2/wildlife/the-canvey-island-monster [Accessed: September 17, 2023].

Hewitt, L. (2016). "Carnivorous Plants: Legends of Man-Eating Flora." [online] *Historic Mysteries.* Available at: https://www.historicmysteries.com/carnivorous-plants/ [Accessed: 2019].

Hume, N. (2014). "Boo Hag." [blog] *The Paranormal Guide.* November 3, 2014. Available at: http://www.theparanormalguide.com/blog/boo-hag [Accessed: 2019].

Ivanits, L. J. (2015). *Russian Folk Belief.* [electronic book] Routledge. [Originally published in 1989] [Accessed: 2019].

Jackson, W. (2004). "The Use of Unicorn Horn in Medicine." *The Pharmaceutical Journal,* vol. 273. Available at: http://www.rhinoresourcecenter.com/pdf_files/117/1175857420.pdf [Accessed: September 17, 2023].

Janse van Vuuren, R. (2019). "Jengu: the Mermaid from Africa #AtoZChallenge." [online] *Ronel the Mythmaker: Life as a South African Writer.* Available at: https://ronelthemythmaker.wordpress.com/2016/04/12/jengu-the-mermaid-from-africa-atozchallenge/ [Accessed: 2019].

Japanese Mythology & Folklore. (n.d.). "Ningyo Mer-Creatures and the Yao Bikuni Folktale." [blog] *Japanesemythology.wordpress.com.* Available at: https://japanesemythology.wordpress.com/toyota-mahime/ningyo/ [Accessed: 2019].

Johnson, B. (n.d.). "The Kelpie, Mythical Scottish Water Horse." [blog] *Historic UK: The History and Heritage Accommodation Guide.* Available at: https://www.historic-uk.com/CultureUK/The-Kelpie/ [Accessed: 2019].

Jones, L. (2015). "Is the Himalayan Yeti a real animal?" [online] *BBC.co.uk.* Available at: http://www.bbc.co.uk/earth/story/20150630-is-there-such-a-thing-as-a-yeti.

Jung, A.R. (2018). "Mythical Creature, 'The Al-mi'raj,' A Horned Rabbit from Arabic Poetry—with Writing Prompt." [online] *ARJungWriter.com.* Available at: https://arjungwriter.com/2018/06/18/mythical-creature-the-al-miraj-a-horned-rabbit-from-arabic-poetry-with-writing-prompt/.

Krystek, L. (2003). "Man Eating Plants." [online] *The Museum of UnNatural Mystery.* Available at: http://www.unmuseum.org/maneatp.htm [Accessed: 2019].

Lamoureux, A. (2018). "This Sloth Monster Is Said to Roam the Amazon Rainforest–Here's What the Evidence Says." [online] *All That's Interesting.* Available at: https://allthatsinteresting.com/mapinguari [Accessed: 2019].

Laskow, S. (2015). "The Mythical Man-Eating Plants That Paved the Way for 'Little Shop of Horrors.'" [online] *Atlas Obscura.* Available at: https://www.atlasobscura.com/articles/the-mythical-maneating-plants-that-paved-the-way-for-little-shop-of-horrors [Accessed: 2019].

Last Podcast on the Left. (2017). "Episode 259: The Puerto Rican Chupacabra." [podcast] The Last Podcast Network. Available at: https://open.spotify.com/episode/7vdcNWfvKec64aQwcpQdQT.

Last Podcast on the Left. (2018). "Episode 314: The Jersey Devil." [podcast] The Last Podcast Network. Available at: https://open.spotify.com/episode/23gsRhg79Pz5Jj2FmtT5kK.

Lighty, C. (2015). "The Crawfordsville Monster." [blog] *Hoosier State Chronicles: Indiana's Digital Historic Newspaper Program.* October 26, 2015. Available at: https://blog.newspapers.library.in.gov/crawfordsville-monster/ [Accessed: 2019].

Little, B. (2018). "How the Bigfoot Legend Began." [online] *History*. Available at: https://www.history.com/news/bigfoot-legend-newspaper [Last modified July 25, 2023] [Accessed: 2019].

Little, B. (2019). "Bigfoot Was Investigated by the FBI. Here's What They Found." [online] *History*. Available at: https://www.history.com/news/bigfoot-fbi-file-investigation-discovery [Last modified June 26, 2023] [Accessed: 2019].

Livingstone, G. and Hendren, T. (2017). *Re-visioning Medusa: From Monster to Divine Wisdom*. Self-published, CreateSpace Independent Publishing Platform.

Lloyd, E. (2016). "Herne the Hunter–The Horned God and Lord of the Forest in British Mythology." [online] *Ancient Pages*. Available at: http://www.ancientpages.com/2016/01/12/herne-hunter-horned-god-lord-forest-british-mythology/ [Accessed: 2019].

Lloyd, E. (2020). "Surprising End to Legend of the Snallygaster That Terrorized Maryland and Washington." [online] *Ancient Pages*. Available at: http://www.ancientpages.com/2018/03/28/surprising-end-to-legend-of-the-snallygaster-that-terrorized-maryland-and-washington/ [Accessed: September 17, 2023].

McCormick, K. (n.d.). "Dragon Species: Tatzelwurm / Tazelwurm / Stollenwurm / Arassas / Bergstutzen / Springwurm / Daazelwurm / Praatzelwurm." [online] *The Circle of the Dragon*. Available at: http://www.blackdrago.com/species/tazelwurm.htm [Last modified October 9, 2017] [Accessed: 2019].

Merriam-Webster, s.v. "Cryptozoology." [online] Available at: https://www.merriam-webster.com/dictionary/cryptozoology [Accessed: July 2023].

Merriam-Webster.com, s.v. "Grimalkin." [online] Available at: https://www.merriam-webster.com/dictionary/grimalkin [Accessed: 2019].

Meyer, M. (2019). "Bakekujira."[online] *Yokai.com: The Online Database of Japanese Folklore*. Available at: http://yokai.com/bakekujira/ [Accessed: 2019].

Meyer, M. (2019). "Gashadokuro."[online] *Yokai.com: The Online Database of Japanese Folklore*. Available at: http://yokai.com/gashadokuro/ [Accessed: 2019].

Meyer, M. (2023). "Waniguchi."[online] *Yokai.com: The Online Database of Japanese Folklore*. Available at: http://yokai.com/waniguchi/ [Accessed: March 2023].

Millward, E. (2014). "Herne the Hunter: A May Day Figure of Folklore." [online] *Shakespeare Birthplace Trust*. Available at: https://www.shakespeare.org.uk/explore-shakespeare/blogs/herne-hunter-may-day-figure-folklore/ [Accessed: 2019].

Montenegro, B. (2015). "The Aswang Diaspora: Why Philippine Lower Myths Continue to Endure." [online] *GMA News Online*. Available at: https://www.gmanetwork.com/news/scitech/technology/535657/the-aswang-diaspora-why-philippine-lower-myths-continue-to-endure/story/ [Accessed: 2019].

Moore, M. (2008). "Montauk Monster: Mystery Animal Corpse Becomes Web Sensation." [online] *The Telegraph*. Available at: https://www.telegraph.co.uk/news/newstopics/howaboutthat/2484017/Montauk-Monster-Mystery-animal-corpse-becomes-web-sensation.html.

Morphy, R. (2010). "Enfield Horror (Illinois, USA)." [online] *Cryptopia: Exploring the Hidden World*. Available at: https://www.cryptopia.us/site/2010/03/enfield-horror-illinois-usa/ [Accessed: 2019].

The Mothman of Point Pleasant. (2017). [film] Directed by S. Breedlove. Produced by Small Town Monsters.

Mowbray, S. (2018). "Meet the Tatzelwurm, Switzerland's Nightmarish 7-Foot Lizard." [online] *Culture Trip*. Available at: https://theculturetrip.com/europe/switzerland/articles/meet-the-tatzelwurm-switzerlands-nightmarish-7-foot-lizard/ [Accessed: 2019].

Mudge, R. (2015). "Meet the 'King of Cats' From Celtic Folklore." [online] *Catster*. Available at: https://www.catster.com/lifestyle/cats-celtic-folklore-scottish-wildcat-cait-sidhe-sith-samhain-halloween [Accessed: 2019].

Mythical-Creatures-and-Beasts.com. (2022). "Cu Sith." [online] Available at: https://www.mythical-creatures-and-beasts.com/cu-sith.html [Accessed: 2019].

Mythicalrealm.com.(2012). "Leviathan: Giant Sea Monsters of Myth and Legend." [online] Available at: http://mythicalrealm.com/creatures/leviathan.html [Accessed: 2019].

Nadel, D. (2018). "The Ningen: Monster of the Antarctic." [online] *Exemplore*. Available at: https://exemplore.com/cryptids/Ningen-Monster-of-the-Antarctic [Last modified July 28, 2022] [Accessed: 2019].

Nadel, D. (2019). "Three Cat Cryptids: White Death, Wampus Beast, and Cactus Cat." [online] *Exemplore*. Available at: https://exemplore.com/cryptids/Three-Cat-Cryptids-White-Death-Wampus-Beast-and-Cactus-Cat [Last modified July 31, 2022].

Newsweek Special Edition. (2015). "A Guide to Deciphering the Differences Between a Yeti, Sasquatch, Bigfoot and More." [online] Newsweek. Available at: https://www.newsweek.com/bigfoot-sasquatch-yeti-legend-myth-403932 [Accessed: 2019].

Newton, M. (2009). *Hidden Animals: A Field Guide to Batsquatch, Chupacabra and Other Elusive Creatures*. Santa Barbara: ABC-CLIO.

Opala, J. A. (n.d.). "The Gullah: Rice, Slavery, and the Sierra Leone-American Connection." [online] *Gilder Lehrman Center for the Study of Slavery, Resistance, and Abolition*. Yale University. Available at: https://glc.yale.edu/sites/default/files/files/Gullah%20Customs%20and%20traditions.pdf [Accessed: 2019].

Paranormal-encyclopedia.com, s.v. "Bunyip." [online] Available at: https://www.paranormal-encyclopedia.com/b/bunyip/ [Accessed: 2019].

Parker, J. (2018). *The Mythic Chinese Unicorn*. Friesen Press, 2nd Edition.

Pearson, A. (2011). "Be Warned: You Are Going to Be Amazed." [online] *Stuff*. Available at: https://www.stuff.co.nz/nelson-mail/4910290/Be-warned-You-are-going-to-be-amazed.

Potgieter, F. (2019). *Psoglav, It goes growl in the night—Frances Potgieter*. [online] Frances Potgieter. Available at: http://francespotgieter.com/psoglav-goes-growl-night/ [Accessed: 2019].

Prior, S. (1939). *Carnivorous Plants and "The Man-Eating Tree."* Chicago: Field Museum of Natural History.

Qian, Z. (2017). "Mythical Birds." [online] *ShanghaiDaily.com*. Available at: https://archive.shine.cn/sunday/now-and-then/Mythical-Birds/shdaily.shtml.

Radford, B. (2014). "Globsters: Mysterious Marine Monster Masses." [online] *Live Science*. Available at: https://www.livescience.com/45780-globsters.html.

Radford, B. (2014). "Mongolian Death Worm: Elusive Legend of the Gobi Desert." [online] *Live Science*. Available at: https://www.livescience.com/46450-mongolian-death-worm.html.

Rafferty, R. (2021). "The Myths and Legends of Ireland's Hound of the Deep, the Dobhar Chu." [online] *Irishcentral.com*. Available at: https://www.irishcentral.com/irelands-hound-of-the-deep-dobhar-chu.

Rainforest Cruises. (2013). "Bigfoot of the Amazon Jungle: The Mapinguari." [blog] April 25, 2013. Available at: https://www.rainforestcruises.com/jungle-blog/bigfoot-of-the-amazon-the-mapinguari.

Redfern, N. (2015). *Chupacabra Road Trip: In Search of the Elusive Beast*. Llewellyn Publications.

Redfern, N. (2019). "Seeking the Sinister Shug Monkey."[online] *Mysterious Universe*. Available at: https://mysteriousuniverse.org/2012/09/seeking-the-sinister-shug-monkey/ [Accessed: 2019].

Rhinelander: Live the Legend. (n.d.). "What's the Hodag?" [online] Available at: https://explorerhinelander.com/whats-the-hodag/ [Accessed: March 2023].

Roberts, M. (2014). "Bastards of the Bestiary: Eight Mythological Creatures Too Gross, Sad, or Monstrous to Be Loved." [online] *Atlas Obscura.* Available at: https://www.atlasobscura.com/articles/magical-mythical-beings [Accessed: 2019].

Rohter, L. (2007). "A Huge Amazon Monster Is Only a Myth. Or Is It?" [online] *The New York Times.* Available at: https://www.nytimes.com/2007/07/08/world/americas/08amazon.html.

Russell, D. (1998). "Roswell Rods." [online] *X-Project Paranormal Magazine.* Available at: http://xprojectmagazine.com/archives/cryptozoology/rods.html.

Saunders, J. M. (2016). "Monster Monday: Psoglav." [blog] January 25, 2016. *Write Wrote Written: The Website of J. Matthew Saunders.* Available at: https://writewrotewritten.wordpress.com/2016/01/25/monster-monday-psoglav/.

Schratt, M. (2011). "Roswell Revelation: The Secret of Hangar P-3." [online] *Open Minds: Credible UFO News and Information.* Available at: https://www.openminds.tv/roswell-secret-of-hangar-p-3/10472.

Schwartz, R. (2012). "The Canvey Island Monster." [online] *Stranger Dimensions.* Available at: https://www.strangerdimensions.com/2012/02/22/the-canvey-island-monster/ [Last modified April 10, 2023].

ScotClans.com. (2013). "The Bean Nighe." [online] Available at: https://www.scotclans.com/pages/the-bean-nighe [Accessed: 2019].

Scotsman, The. (2016). "Scottish Myths: Wulver the Kindhearted Shetland Werewolf." [online] Available at: https://www.scotsman.com/news/people/scottish-myths-wulver-the-kindhearted-shetland-werewolf-2463904.

Shannon, L. (2017). "Medusa and Athena: Ancient Allies in Healing Women's Trauma." [blog] *Feminism and Religion.* June 24, 2017. Available at:https://feminismandreligion.com/2017/06/24/medusa-and-athena-ancient-allies-in-healing-womens-trauma-by-laura-shannon.

Sharpe, L. S. (2019). "Museum Library." [online] *Lumberwoods: Unnatural History Museum.* Available at: http://www.lib.lumberwoods.org/.

Spence, L. (2016). *Hero Tales and Legends of the Rhine.* [classic reprint] FORGOTTEN Books. (Originally published in 1915).

Stockton, C. (2018). *12 Creepy Facts about the Dover Demon.* [online] *Thought Catalog.* Available at: https://thoughtcatalog.com/christine-stockton/2018/07/dover-demon/ [Accessed: 2019].

Sullivan, K. (2016). "Rusalka: The Mythical Slavic Mermaid." [online] *Ancient Origins*. Available at. https://www.ancient-origins.net/myths-legends/rusalka-mythical-slavic-mermaid-006738.

Sutherland, A. (2016). "Leshy: Master of Forest and Wildlife in Slavic Beliefs." [online] *Ancient Pages*. Available at: http://www.ancientpages.com/2016/03/25/leshy-master-of-forest-and-wildlife-in-slavic-beliefs/.

Swancer, B. (2016). "The Strange Case of the Enfield Horror." [online] *Mysterious Universe*. Available at: https://mysteriousuniverse.org/2016/02/the-strange-case-of-the-enfield-horror/ [Accessed: 2019].

Swancer, B. (2018). "The Mysterious Monster Of the Deep Blue Holes of the Bahamas." [online] *Mysterious Universe*. Available at: https://mysteriousuniverse.org/2018/04/the-mysterious-monster-of-the-deep-blue-holes-of-the-bahamas/ [Accessed: 2019].

Sweeney, M. (2014). "The Enfield Horror." [online] *The Paranormal Guide*. Available at: http://www.theparanormalguide.com/blog/the-enfield-horror.

Szczepanski, K. (2019). "What Is a Qilin?" [online] *ThoughtCo*. Available at: https://www.thoughtco.com/what-is-a-qilin-195005.

Topham, I. (2008). "Will o' the Wisp."[online] *Mysterious Britain & Ireland: Mysteries, Legends & the Paranormal*. Available at: http://www.mysteriousbritain.co.uk/folklore/will-o-the-wisp/ [Last modified December 3, 2018].

Torjussen, S. (2016). "'Release the Kraken!'—The Recontextualization of the Kraken in Popular Culture, from *Clash of the Titans* to *Magic: The Gathering*." [online] *New Voices in Classical Reception Studies*, vol. 11. Available at: https://brage.inn.no/inn-xmlui/handle/11250/2424600.

Towrie, S. (n.d.). "The Selkie Folk of Orkney Folklore." [online] *Orkneyjar: The Heritage of the Orkney Islands*. Available at: http://www.orkneyjar.com/folklore/selkiefolk/ [Last modified in 2023].

Tréguer, P. (2016). "The Origin and Various Meanings of 'Grimalkin.'" [blog] *Word Histories*. November 30, 2016. Available at: https://wordhistories.net/2016/11/30/grimalkin/.

Unknownexplorers.com. (2006). "Dobhar-Chu." [online] Available at: http://www.unknownexplorers.com/dobharchu.php.

Upton, E. (2013). "What Causes Will-o'-the-Wisps." [online] *Today I Found Out: Feed Your Brain*. Available at: http://www.todayifoundout.com/index.php/2013/04/what-causes-will-o-the-wisps/.

Urswick, L. (2019). "Mapinguari Sightings: Evidence the Giant Ground Sloth Is Still Alive?" [online] *Exemplore*. Available at: https://exemplore.com/cryptids/Mapinguari-Sightings-Does-Mylodon-Still-Exist [Last modified February 2, 2023].

Van De Casteele, A. (2014). "Who is Bean Nighe, Celtic Washerwoman, Prophetess of Doom?" [online] *Spooky Isles*. Available at: https://www.spookyisles.com/2014/07/bean-nighe-celtic-washerwoman/.

Van Doren Honeyman, A. (1918). *Documents Relating to the Colonial History of the State Of New Jersey*, XXX [online]. Available at: https://archive.org/details/calendarnewjers00edgoog/page/294/mode/2up.

von Radowitz, J. (2017). "Does Prehistoric Otter Explain Dobhar-chú Myth?" [online] *Independent.ie*. Available at: https://www.independent.ie/irish-news/does-prehistoric-otter-explain-dobharch-myth-36306533.html.

Wayland, E. and Wayland, T. (2017). "The Dover Demon." [online] *The Singular Fortean Society*. Available at: https://www.singularfortean.com/singularjournal/2017/11/13/the-dover-demon.

Windsor Berkshire. (n.d.). "Herne the Hunter." [online] Available at: https://www.windsor-berkshire.co.uk/herne-the-hunter/ [Accessed: 2019].

Winters, R. (2016). "Legends of the Selkies, Hidden Gems of Sea Mythology." [online] *AncientOrigins*. Available at: https://www.ancient-origins.net/myths-legends/legends-selkies-hidden-germs-sea-mythology-006409.

Wunderkabinett.blogspot.com. (2014). "Lepus Cornutus—Jackalopes, Wolpherfingers, Skvaders." [blog] February 7, 2014. Available at: http://wunderkabinett.blogspot.com/2014/02/the-actual-history-of-antlered-rabbits.html.